P9-BYK-317

RACHEL CARSON

Conservation Heroes

Ansel Adams
John James Audubon
Rachel Carson
Jacques Cousteau
Jane Goodall
Al Gore
Steve and Bindi Irwin
Chico Mendes
John Muir
Theodore Roosevelt

Conservation Heroes

RACHEL CARSON

Marie-Therese Miller

CHELSEA HOUSE
An Infobase Learning Company

Rachel Carson

Copyright ©2011 by Infobase Learning

All rights reserved. No part of this book may be reproduced or utilized in any form or by any means, electronic or mechanical, including photocopying, recording, or by any information storage or retrieval systems, without permission in writing from the publisher. For information, contact:

Chelsea House
An imprint of Infobase Learning
132 West 31st Street
New York, NY 10001

Library of Congress Cataloging-in-Publication Data
Miller, Marie-Therese.
  Rachel Carson / by Marie-Therese Miller.
      p. cm. — (Conservation heroes)
  Includes bibliographical references and index.
  ISBN 978-1-60413-950-1 (hardcover)
1. Carson, Rachel, 1907–1964—Juvenile literature. 2. Biologists—United States—Biography—Juvenile literature. 3. Environmentalists—United States—Biography—Juvenile literature. 4. Science writers—United States—Biography—Juvenile literature. I. Title.
  QH31.C33M55 2011
  333.95'16092—dc22
  [B]   2010030596

Chelsea House books are available at special discounts when purchased in bulk quantities for businesses, associations, institutions, or sales promotions. Please call our Special Sales Department in New York at (212) 967-8800 or (800) 322-8755.

You can find Chelsea House on the World Wide Web
at http://www.chelseahouse.com

Text design by Annie O'Donnell
Cover design by Takeshi Takaheshi
Composition by Newgen North America
Cover printed by Bang Printing, Brainerd, MN
Book printed and bound by Bang Printing, Brainerd, MN
Date printed: February 2011
Printed in the United States of America

10 9 8 7 6 5 4 3 2 1

This book is printed on acid-free paper.

All links and Web addresses were checked and verified to be correct at the time of publication. Because of the dynamic nature of the Web, some addresses and links may have changed since publication and may no longer be valid.

Contents

Silent Spring Causes an Uproar

Rachel Carson was a marine biologist, ecologist, conservation-ist, and an award-winning author. She wrote books about the ocean that clearly explained scientific ideas and captured the imagination of her readers. The book for which she is most well known is *Silent Spring,* which sounded the alarm about the dangers pesticides posed to wildlife. *Silent Spring* is credited with starting the modern environmental movement.

EARLY OBSERVATIONS

Carson grew up in Springdale, Pennsylvania, where she spent much of her time outdoors observing mammals, birds, insects, and flowers with her mother. She loved nature, and she loved to write.

The Carson home was located only 14 miles (22.5 kilometers) from the city of Pittsburgh, Pennsylvania. Carson could see that the factories in Pittsburgh emitted smoke into the air and pumped waste into the rivers. From a young age, Carson witnessed how peo-ple were poisoning the environment.

Rachel Carson poses in this 1951 image. By this time, the 44-year-old had written two books, *Under the Sea Wind* and *The Sea Around Us,* and she continued to be concerned about the dangers posed by pesticides.

Carson earned a bachelor's degree in biology from Pennsylvania College for Women and a master's degree in zoology from The Johns Hopkins University. She then became a government scientist for the U.S. Bureau of Fisheries (later called the U.S. Fish and Wildlife Service).

Carson's work with the government gave her access to information ordinary scientists didn't have. She knew that during

HEINZ MENG AND THE PEREGRINE FALCONS

Peregrine falcons are raptors, birds of prey, and have excellent eyesight and sharp talons and beaks. They have nesting places on rock cliffs and hunt in open spaces during the day. Peregrine falcons dive down to strike their bird prey in mid-air. These dives, or stoops, can reach speeds up to 200 miles (322 km) per hour. Peregrines hit their prey with their taloned feet and use their beaks to sever the prey's spinal cord.

By the 1960s, peregrine falcons had disappeared completely from the eastern United States, and only 15 percent of the population remained west of the Mississippi River. DDT was to blame. DDT concentrates as it moves up the food chain. Peregrines are at the high end of the food chain, so they ingest large concentrations of DDT.

The DDT in the peregrines' bodies changed to DDE (dichlorodiphenyldichloroethylene), which affected the females' reproductive systems. As a result, the eggs they laid had shells that were too thin. These eggshells would crack easily on the rock cliffs of the nesting places, and the young raptors would not survive.

Dr. Heinz Meng's fascination with raptors began when he was a young man, and he became an avid falconer. He earned his doctorate in ornithology from Cornell University. Meng's admiration for raptors motivated him to step in to save the disappearing peregrine falcon population. He decided to try to breed peregrines in captivity and then release the offspring into the wild. He trapped two young peregrines on their first southern migration. These are called passage peregrines. However, these raptors refused to breed in captivity. Meng thought perhaps they were already too used to the wild to be comfortable breeding in captivity.

(continues)

(continued)

Instead, he thought that if young peregrines were taken from a nesting place before they could fly, they might breed in captivity. He obtained a pair of these raptors from British Columbia in 1967.

When these peregrines reached breeding age, they produced a live offspring. However, they did not know how to care for the young raptor, so Meng fed it. These peregrines produced more live offspring. Over time, they learned how to feed their young successfully.

Meng realized that the breeding needed to be done on a larger scale. Cornell University's Laboratory of Ornithology agreed to take over the breeding program, and Meng donated his breeding pair to the university. Meng made certain that the peregrines bred in captivity did not have much contact with humans. If humans play too big a role, the birds become tame and trusting of people. Then the raptors cannot be released safely into the wild because they would not have the necessary hunting skills to survive or a healthy fear of human beings with guns.

Meng succeeded in releasing the peregrines bred in captivity into the wild. The peregrine population gradually increased. As of August 25, 1999, the peregrine falcon was taken off the federal threatened and endangered species list. About 10 percent of the peregrines in the United States can be traced back to Meng's original breeding pair. "Again the high cliffs . . . and many other silent places will ring once more to the sharp, clear call of the peregrine, returned to live among us," wrote Meng and John Kaufman in their 1992 book, *Falcons Return: Restoring an Endangered Species.*

World War II, the military was using the pesticide dichloro-diphenyltrichloroethane (DDT) to kill insects that carried disease. After the war, DDT was sold to civilians to use. DDT and other pesticides were still used to kill insects that transmitted disease.

They were also used to control insects and plants that destroyed crops.

Carson and her colleagues at the U.S. Fish and Wildlife Service (FWS) became concerned that pesticides were not only eliminating the targeted insects and plants but also killing other wildlife. In 1945, she asked the editors of *Reader's Digest* if they wanted her to write an article about the negative effects of DDT; however, the magazine editors were not interested in publishing the article. They believed, along with most of the public, that chemical pesticides were wonderful discoveries.

In the late 1950s, frightening events were occurring. Birds, fish, and livestock were being killed by pesticides, and people were being sickened. Carson decided to write a whole book to warn the public about the hazards of pesticide use. That book was *Silent Spring.*

The New Yorker magazine published portions of *Silent Spring* before it became a book. The first part ran on June 2, 1962. Then, Houghton Mifflin published *Silent Spring* on September 27, 1962.

In *Silent Spring,* Carson wrote about the effects of pesticides on air, water, and soil. She gave examples of the killing of wildlife by pesticides. She also linked pesticides to cancer and genetic damage in humans. Carson called for more research into the effects of pesticides. She hoped to see a reduction in pesticide use, especially in those—like DDT—that lasted a long time in the environment. She suggested biological alternatives to pesticides, such as using natural predators to destroy targeted insects.

Silent Spring received positive reviews. It was popular with readers and became Number 1 on *The New York Times* Best Seller List. Carson even received a letter of praise from author E.B. White. Dr. Albert Schweitzer sent her a note of thanks for dedicating *Silent Spring* to him. That note became one of Carson's most prized possessions.

The Book-of-the-Month Club chose the book for its October selection. Carson was pleased that people in rural areas across the country would now have access to *Silent Spring* and its message. She wrote her friend Dorothy Freeman, "And the BOM [Book-of-the-Month Club] will carry it to farms and hamlets all over the country that don't know what a bookstore looks like—much less *The New Yorker.* So it is very, very good and tonight I am deeply and quietly happy."

THE CRITICS REACT

Not surprisingly, the executives at the chemical companies that made pesticides were angry about the contents of *Silent Spring.* They were worried that the book would convince the public to stop using pesticides. They were also concerned that the government would step in and limit pesticide use. The National Agricultural Chemicals Association, a pesticide trade group, put $250,000—a whole quarter of a million dollars—toward a campaign to discredit *Silent Spring.*

Velsicol Chemical Company of Chicago made chlordane and heptachlor, pesticides specifically mentioned in *Silent Spring.* The company contacted *The New Yorker* and Houghton Mifflin and threatened to sue if Carson's facts were incorrect. Neither the magazine nor the publishing company was intimidated. They supported Carson and published her writing. Velsicol finally backed off because Carson's work was well supported by solid research.

Many people viewed pesticides as beneficial to the world. They killed disease-bearing insects, such as mosquitoes that transmitted malaria. Pesticides also helped farmers stop insects and weeds from destroying crops, so people had more food to eat.

Carson's critics thought that *Silent Spring* might end pesticide use. They predicted awful consequences if pesticides were banned. William Darby, head of biochemistry at Vanderbilt School of Medicine, said that a world without pesticides "means disease, epidemics, starvation, misery and suffering." The Monsanto Company published a pamphlet titled "The Desolate World," which described how terrible life would be without pesticides.

The magazine *American Agriculturist* ran a satirical story about what might happen if pesticides were outlawed. In the tale, an author had written a book calling for the ban of all pesticides. The country's government followed the author's suggestion and stopped pesticide use. A boy and his grandfather sat alone in the country's forest. The boy's mother had died of insect-borne malaria. His dad had died during a famine because grasshoppers had destroyed the crops. The boy and his grandfather would soon die of starvation. Meanwhile, it was noted that the author of the imaginary book, who had made lots of money from the sale of the book and had moved to a country that still had pesticides, was doing just fine.

Carson's critics, however, had not read her book carefully enough. Carson had not recommended the end of all pesticide use. She understood that pesticides were helpful in fighting disease and in growing food. Carson wanted pesticide use reduced and for more safety testing to be done on the pesticides.

Critics not only attacked the ideas in *Silent Spring* but also took aim at Carson personally. Some mocked her as a nature nut and implied she was being hysterical.

Her scientific credentials were questioned. Carson was educated as a biologist. At that time in history, biology was looked down upon as a lesser science; chemistry was king.

In addition, Carson had never earned her doctorate. Dr. Robert White-Stevens, the assistant director of the Agricultural Research Division of American Cyanamid, was one of her most vocal critics. He made sure to refer to Carson as "Miss Carson," so that listeners knew that she didn't have a Ph.D.

Many of the comments made about Carson were anti-woman. One particularly anti-female remark is often attributed to Ezra Taft Benson, the former secretary of agriculture. In *Silent Spring*, Carson wrote that pesticides could damage human genes. Benson wrote to President Dwight Eisenhower that Carson was "a spinster. What's she so worried about genetics for?" He added that she was "probably a Communist."

President John F. Kennedy took notice of *Silent Spring*. On August 29, 1962, a reporter asked him if government agencies were looking into the possible dangers of pesticides. "Yes, and I know that they already are," Kennedy answered. "I think particularly, of course, since Miss Carson's book, but they are examining the matter."

President Kennedy had his President's Science Advisory Committee consider the effects of pesticides. The committee asked Carson to share her expertise about pesticides. She testified before the committee on January 26, 1963.

The television show *CBS Reports* with host Eric Sevareid invited Carson to appear on the program to share her views about pesticide use. Dr. White-Stevens would be on the show to offer the opposing position. The show also included government officials who had a direct interest in pesticides; those who were concerned about pesticides as they related to health—the U.S. surgeon general and the chief toxicologist for the Public Health Service; and those who viewed pesticide use from the food production standpoint—the U.S. secretary of agriculture and the commissioner of the U.S. Food and Drug Administration. A representative from the President's Science Advisory Committee was on hand, too.

It is interesting to note that before the program was broadcast on April 3, 1963, three out of the five commercial sponsors for the show withdrew. Lehn and Fink (the makers of Lysol) and food companies Standard Brands, Inc. and Ralston Purina did not want their names associated with a controversial program about pesticides. However, CBS went ahead with the program. With fewer commercial breaks, there was more time for the experts to speak.

Carson was very ill when she was interviewed for *CBS Reports*. She was battling breast cancer that had spread throughout her body. Even though she was physically weak, Carson was strong intellectually. She knew her material and made her points clearly and effectively. The debate concluded in her favor.

On May 15, 1963, the President's Science Advisory Committee published its report, "Use of Pesticide." The report supported Carson's position on pesticide use. Sevareid went on the air with a follow-up program to discuss the committee's findings. "Miss Carson had two immediate aims," he said. "One was to alert the

In this November 1962 image, Rachel Carson is interviewed by CBS-TV journalist Eric Sevareid about her book, *Silent Spring,* in the study of her Maryland home.

public; the second, to build a fire under the Government. She accomplished the first aim a month ago. Tonight's report by the President's panel is *prima facie* [at first sight] evidence that she has accomplished the second."

Carson was called upon to testify before a Senate subcommittee headed by Senator Abraham Ribicoff of Connecticut, and she appeared on June 4, 1963. Carson shared many recommendations with the committee. Among other things, she suggested reduction in the use of long-lasting pesticides and more research into effects of pesticides. She wished to see strict controls imposed on aerial

(continues on page 18)

AL GORE AND RACHEL CARSON

Rachel Carson's book *Silent Spring* is often credited with beginning the modern environmental movement. Today's environmental movement seeks to make sure Earth and its inhabitants are healthy. Participants work to reduce pollution in the air, water, and soil. They encourage people to conserve natural resources and to recycle and reuse items. The environmental movement encompasses everything from saving the polar bears to using more energy-efficient light bulbs.

Rachel Carson's *Silent Spring* inspired not only the environmental movement but also one of its most visible members, former vice president Al Gore. Gore said that when he was young, he and his entire family read *Silent Spring*. For weeks, they had lively dinner table discussions about the book. Gore said that Carson influenced him in his own environmental work. He even had a picture of Carson on his office wall when he was vice president.

Gore wrote the introduction to the 1994 reissue of *Silent Spring*. In the introduction he wrote about Carson, "Her work, the truth she brought to light, the science and research she inspired, stand not only as powerful arguments for limiting the use of pesticides but as powerful proof of the difference that one individual can make."

Gore is another individual making a difference. He is concerned with global climate change, the temperature increase of the air near Earth's surface and bodies of water. Global climate change is caused by a buildup of greenhouse gases resulting from the burning of fossil fuels. In addition to other books about the environment, Gore wrote the 2006 book *An Inconvenient Truth: The Planetary Emergency of Global Warming and What We Can Do About It*. The book explains global climate change and suggests steps that

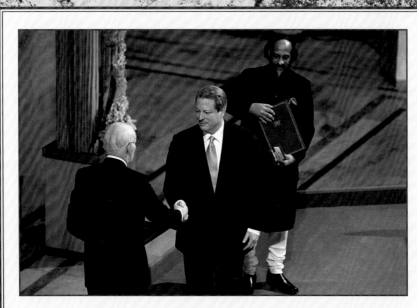

Former vice president Al Gore receives the Nobel Peace Prize in Oslo, Norway, on December 10, 2007. On the right is Rajendra Pachauri, representing the Intergovernmental Panel on Climate Change. In his speech, Gore urged the world to increase efforts to combat climate change.

people can take to reduce their consumption of fossil fuels. His film about climate change, *An Inconvenient Truth,* won the 2007 Academy Award for best documentary feature.

As vice president, Gore helped negotiate the Kyoto Protocol—an agreement signed by nations that committed to limiting greenhouse gases. The Kyoto Protocol was adopted on December 11, 1997.

Gore and the Intergovernmental Panel on Climate Change shared the 2007 Nobel Peace Prize. The prize was awarded in recognition of their work educating the public about climate change and for outlining solutions to counteract this environmental threat.

(continued from page 15)

pesticide spraying. She encouraged the use of biological alternatives to chemical pesticides.

Carson's book *Silent Spring* would alert the public to the harm pesticides could do to the environment. Her insightful words would echo for years to come.

The Early Years

Rachel Louise Carson was born on May 27, 1907 to Maria and Robert Carson. She had two older siblings ready to welcome her, 10-year-old Marian and 8-year-old Robert.

The Carson family lived on nearly 65 acres (26.3 hectares) in Springdale, Pennsylvania. The property was 14 miles (22.5 km) northeast of Pittsburgh and close to the banks of the Allegheny River. Their modest clapboard house had only four rooms: a parlor and dining room on the first floor and two bedrooms upstairs. The kitchen was located in a lean-to built onto the rear of the home and had only a dirt floor. A fruit cellar under the house could be reached from an outdoor entrance.

The home did not have central heat but was kept warm by two chimneys and a small coal stove in each room. The house had electrical wiring for some ceiling fixtures. Because there was no indoor plumbing, there were two outhouses on the property. Fresh water was available from a springhouse built into the hillside 50 feet (15.2 meters) from the residence. The cool temperature of the springhouse also made this area useful for refrigerating perishables.

The Carsons had some animals, including a horse, cows, chickens, dogs, and cats. They used the horse and a buggy to run

This early (circa 1910) image of Rachel Carson shows her sitting on her mother Maria's lap. Her sister Marian and brother Robert are also pictured.

errands in town. The property consisted of wooded areas, rolling open spaces, and an apple orchard. The townspeople referred to the orchard as Carson's Grove. The Carsons sold fruit from the orchard to make a bit of extra money, and often neighbors could be found picnicking among the apple trees. Maria Carson planted a large garden to have fresh produce for the family table.

Rachel's father, however, had not purchased the land to be used as a working farm. He hoped that people living and working in Pittsburgh would want to move from the city to the rural setting of Springdale. He planned to make money by dividing his acreage into smaller plots and selling them to those people. Unfortunately, city dwellers did not flock to Springdale, thwarting his goal of becoming wealthy.

Rachel's dad worked for an insurance company and traveled often. Her sister and brother were in school all day, so Rachel and her mother, Maria, spent hours alone together. The two formed a close bond.

Maria had a great love of and respect for nature, which she shared with Rachel. Much of their time together was spent exploring the outdoors. In an article in *The Saturday Review of Literature,* Maria remembered that she taught her daughter "as a tiny child joy in the out-of-doors and the lore of birds, insects and residents of streams and ponds." They also studied plants together. Rachel remembered that on one of her nature walks she found a fossilized fish. This discovery started her wondering about the sea and its inhabitants.

Rachel was permitted to bring creatures home to study them, but Maria instructed her to return them to their natural habitat when she finished. Rachel took this lesson to heart and practiced it for the rest of her life.

Maria instilled an enthusiasm for the natural world in Rachel and encouraged her along the path that would become her life's work. As an adult, Rachel would recall in a letter to *Outdoor Life* editor Raymond Brown: "As long as I can remember, I have been interested in the world of nature, in wild creatures, and in natural unspoiled beauty."

The Carson family did not own a television set or a radio. In the evenings, they would entertain themselves by singing, playing the piano, and reading to one another. Rachel loved to read. Not

THE SMOKY CITY

While she was growing up, Rachel Carson had the chance to observe the way people could negatively affect their environment. In her hometown of Springdale, Rachel could smell the foul odor that polluted the air from the local glue factory. The area electric companies, West Penn Power Company and Duquesne Light Company, burned coal for power, emitting soot from their smokestacks. The nearby city of Pittsburgh also stood as a lesson to Rachel about how industries could pollute the environment.

Pittsburgh was west of the Allegheny Mountains in the southwest corner of Pennsylvania. The city had three rivers: the Allegheny and Monongahela rivers merged to form the Ohio River. The area surrounding Pittsburgh was rich with natural resources, such as lumber, sand for glassmaking, and bituminous coal. The availability of these resources, coupled with the ease of transport provided by the rivers, made Pittsburgh the perfect place for factories. It is interesting to note that Rachel's father was offered money for the coal, which lay under his land. He refused because he didn't want the digging of coal to ruin the natural beauty of his acreage.

In the late 1800s, Pittsburgh's glass factories were the world's largest suppliers of glass. In 1875, Andrew Carnegie, a nineteenth-century industrial giant who helped build the American steel industry, opened his first steel plant in nearby Braddock, Pennsylvania, and by 1911, Pittsburgh's many steel mills were producing as much as half the country's steel. George Westinghouse, inventor of air brakes, also established his factories, including Westinghouse Electric, in the city.

surprisingly, she especially enjoyed stories about animals, such as Beatrix Potter's *The Tale of Peter Rabbit* and *The Wind in the Willows* by Kenneth Grahame.

Most of these factories were coal-powered and polluted the air. The air pollution was so severe that Pittsburgh was called the smoky city. Sometimes, streetlights had to be lit even during the day. The factories dumped waste into the rivers, as well, until they became like open sewers.

Through the early twentieth century, factory pollution was unregulated by the government. In this 1903 image, a group of boys walks up a hill overlooking the Homestead steel plant in Pittsburgh.

Even as a child, Rachel Carson loved animals. In this undated image from her personal collection, she poses with two dogs.

In 1913, Rachel began her formal education at School Street School. She walked the 0.6 mile (0.97 km) to school each day. Rachel was a good student, receiving a grade of A in most subjects, except penmanship. She was quiet and did not make many friends.

Interestingly, attendance records show that Rachel was frequently absent from school. Maria kept her home when the winter weather was bad and when there were outbreaks of childhood diseases, such as measles, diphtheria, or whooping cough. In the early 1900s, no vaccines were available to combat these illnesses, and Maria wanted to keep her daughter well. Despite her absences, Rachel continued to excel at school, thanks to Maria's tutoring.

MARIA CARSON

Maria was prepared to teach Rachel because she had been well educated herself. Maria was the daughter of a Presbyterian minister. After her father died of tuberculosis at age 40, her mother continued to raise Maria and her sister, Ida, alone. Maria attended Washington Female Seminary in Washington, Pennsylvania. The school was a finishing school for young women, but it also offered challenging academic courses, such as Latin.

After graduation, Maria became a teacher. She met Robert Carson at a choral performance in Canonsburg, Pennsylvania, where they were both performing. The two married in June 1894, and Maria stopped teaching. Women of that time period were not permitted to teach after marriage. To help supplement the family finances, Maria offered piano lessons for 50 cents a session.

Maria's early family life gave her an appreciation for how much strong women, like her mother, could accomplish. Her devout Presbyterian upbringing, notes Rachel Carson biographer Mark Hamilton Lytle, offered Maria a respect for nature, an antimaterialistic viewpoint, and an interest in reform, all of which she was able to pass on to Rachel.

A PUBLISHED WRITER

Maria also shared her love of reading with Rachel, and through this enjoyment of books, Rachel found the motivation to write. Rachel would later recall in a speech to female journalists, "I read a great deal almost from infancy and I suppose I must have

(continues on page 28)

ALBERT SCHWEITZER:
REVERENCE FOR LIFE

Both Rachel Carson and her mother, Maria, were admirers of Albert Schweitzer, the philosopher and physician. They were especially interested in the universal ethical principle he created called "reverence for life." Basically, "reverence for life" said that all living things want to continue to live and that everything that lives has that in common. Therefore, people should respect all living things. In his book *The Philosophy of Civilization,* Schweitzer wrote, "A man is truly ethical only when he obeys the compulsion to help all life which he is able to assist, and shrinks from injuring anything that lives."

Carson dedicated her book *Silent Spring* to Schweitzer. When she was presented the Animal Welfare Institute's Albert Schweitzer Award, she said he was "the only truly great individual our modern times has produced."

Albert Schweitzer was born on January 14, 1875, in the Alsace area of what was then Germany. He earned his doctorate of philosophy in 1899 and licentiate in theology in 1900. For years, Schweitzer led a full life. He was a church pastor, an internationally recognized organist, and a college principal. He even authored a biography about Johann Sebastian Bach.

Schweitzer became distressed when he learned that the people of Africa were suffering from a lack of medical care. He returned to school and earned his medical degree in 1913. He and his wife then traveled to Lambaréné in French Equatorial Africa (now Gabon) and founded his hospital.

Schweitzer developed his "reverence for life" principle in 1915. He recalled that he had felt respect for animals since childhood. He even created a special prayer for animals, which he recited each night. Because of his "reverence for life" philosophy, Schweitzer

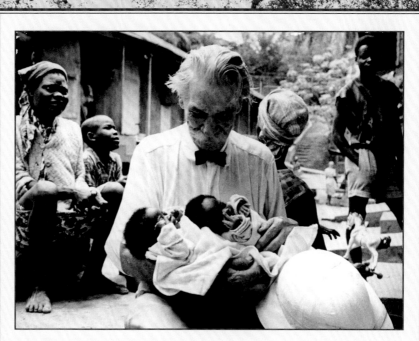

Albert Schweitzer was one of Rachel Carson's heroes. Here, as part of his work as a medical missionary, he holds two newborn babies at the hospital he founded in Lambaréné, French Equatorial Africa (present-day Gabon), in the 1950s.

is often considered a precursor of the environmental and animal welfare movements.

Because the Schweitzers were German citizens working in a French colony during World War I, they were taken to France and interned there during the war. Schweitzer returned to Lambaréné in 1924, where he expanded his hospital to 72 buildings that could hold 600 patients.

In 1953, Schweitzer was awarded the delayed 1952 Nobel Peace Prize. He used the prize money to build a hospital for people with leprosy. Schweitzer continued to oversee his hospital until he died at 90 years of age on September 4, 1965.

(continued from page 25)

realized someone wrote the books, and thought it would be fun to make up stories, too."

Rachel started writing at a young age. At eight years of age, she wrote and illustrated a story called "The Little Brown House." The tale was about a family of wrens in search of the right type of home.

Maria McLean Carson, called "Mamma" by her children, was very close to Rachel Carson and supportive of her work.

The story demonstrated Rachel's fascination with nature and her interest in writing.

Rachel received a monthly magazine called *St. Nicholas*. This magazine contained stories written by well-known children's authors, such as Louisa May Alcott, the author of *Little Women*, and Mark Twain.

St. Nicholas had a section, the *St. Nicholas* League, which accepted and published stories written by children under the age of 18. Each month, the editors of the *St. Nicholas* League awarded worthy stories a Gold Badge for first place or Silver Badge for second place. If a young writer had won both a Gold and a Silver Badge, the writer would be made an Honor Member and be given $10.

When Rachel was only 10 years old, she wrote and submitted a story, "A Battle in the Clouds," to the *St. Nicholas* League. Rachel's brother Robert had joined the Army Air Service during World War I and served in France. He told Rachel the story of a brave Canadian aviator. This tale was the inspiration for her submission.

"A Battle in the Clouds" was about a Canadian aviator who was engaged in a firefight with German flyers. The wing of the Canadian's plane was terribly damaged. The aviator crawled out onto the wing to balance the plane, so it could land safely. The German soldiers were so impressed by his quick thinking and bravery that they did not shoot him when the plane touched down on the ground.

Rachel became a published writer when she was only 11 years old. "A Battle in the Clouds" appeared in the *St. Nicholas* League in September 1918. She was awarded the Silver Badge for it.

Rachel was so encouraged by this writing success that she sent additional stories to *St. Nicholas* League. Her piece "A Message to the Front" was awarded the Gold Badge. Rachel's fourth published work, "A Famous Sea Fight," made her an Honor Member and won her $10 for her efforts.

With her publication in the *St. Nicholas* League, Rachel joined a group of other young people who had stories in the League and would later become well-known authors. Some of these young

In this image, dated circa 1915, young Rachel sits along the
Allegheny River in Pennsylvania with her sister and brother.

writers were E.B. White, author of *Charlotte's Web*; Edna St. Vincent Millay; and F. Scott Fitzgerald.

At age 14, Rachel wrote an article about *St. Nicholas* magazine and submitted it to the periodical. The editors said they couldn't publish it in the magazine but asked to use it for publicity purposes. They paid Rachel one cent per word, for a total of $3. When she received that money, Rachel considered herself a professional writer.

Of course, Rachel's writing was done in her spare time. Her schoolwork was most important to her. She continued as a student at School Street School through tenth grade because her parents could not afford the cost of the daily train needed to transport her to high school.

She transferred to Parnassus High School for eleventh and twelfth grade, which was an inexpensive trolley ride from her home. At Parnassus, Rachel continued to be a top-notch student. She graduated first in her class in 1925.

College Days

Carson chose to attend Pennsylvania College for Women (PCW), now known as Chatham University, in Pittsburgh, Pennsylvania. She was drawn to the school because it was founded on Christian principles and offered a strong academic program.

The college cost $1,000 a year, which was a strain on the Carson family's budget. Carson received a $100 scholarship from the college and another $100 scholarship from the 40th Senatorial District. Her father hoped to pay a portion of the tuition by selling lots of his land. Sending Carson to college was so important to her mother that Maria sold china and silver that she had inherited from her own mother to help pay the college charges. Maria also took on additional piano students.

However, none of the family's sacrifices could meet the educational costs. Fortunately, PCW president Cora Coolidge was impressed with Carson's academic abilities and was able to convince private donors to pay the rest of her annual tuition.

In the 1920s, the career choice of most of the women attending PCW was marriage and motherhood. The purpose of college for these women was to be educated so that they could share knowledge with their children and hold intelligent conversations with their husbands. Some of the PCW students would study toward careers that were open to women, such as teaching and social work. Carson opted to major in English because she dreamed of becoming a writer.

Rachel Carson poses for her 1928 Pennsylvania College for Women yearbook photo.

WOMEN AT WORK

The most acceptable career for a woman in the early 1900s in the United States was that of wife and mother. A woman was considered a natural caretaker. She could act as nurturer and moral compass for the family. Those women who did enter the work force were often domestic servants, still in a position of caring for others in a home setting. Single women who studied toward a profession, such as teaching, were forced back to the home by state laws known as marriage bars. Marriage bars prohibited married women from continuing with certain jobs once they were married. This type of law kept Maria Carson from teaching in school after she wed.

World War I opened the door for women to join the work force because so many men were fighting overseas. These women took jobs in the factories, such as those in the steel and auto industries. They proved that they were competent workers. However, when the men returned from the war, the women had to leave these positions.

Women won the right to vote on August 18, 1920, with the ratification of the Nineteenth Amendment to the U.S. Constitution. With this advancement in women's rights, women gradually gained more opportunities in education and in the workplace.

In the 1920s, more women were working in factories. An increased number of women were graduating from high school, and they were working as clerks in offices, as saleswomen in retail stores, and as employees for the telephone companies.

More women were also attending college. The majority of college-bound women were still hoping to find husbands and marry. Other women were studying to enter professions that were open to women, including teaching, social work, and nursing—the professions in which women nurtured others.

Women like Rachel Carson and Mary Scott Skinker were studying science and entering a male-dominated profession. They were blazing a path for the next generation of women to follow.

At PCW, Carson was as focused on her studies as she had been as a younger student. She did not make many friends. Carson's quiet nature and studiousness were sometimes mistaken for unfriendliness by her college classmates.

Carson's shortage of money hindered her social life. Many of the other students at the college came from families with money. Sometimes, these young women looked down on scholarship recipients like Carson. Carson also lacked the money to attend many of the social activities, such as dances and teas. She didn't have funds to buy appropriate clothes for these events either. To complicate matters, Carson had a severe case of acne, so she shied away from social contact.

Another factor that likely contributed to Carson's trouble forming college friendships was her close relationship with her mother. Carson and her mother had never been separated before, so Maria came to visit her frequently on the weekends. She was eager to share her daughter's college experiences.

Because Carson and her mother spent time together while the other girls were bonding with one another, Carson missed these opportunities to make friends. At times, Carson and her mother were so focused on their relationship that they ignored the other students. Carson's freshman roommate, Dorothy Appleby, remembers that Maria Carson would bring freshly baked cookies to her daughter and neither would think to offer the treats to the other girls.

It is interesting to note that Carson's sophomore year roommate was a young 16-year-old girl named Helen Myers. They roomed together for the next three years. In her 1997 book *Rachel Carson: Witness for Nature,* author Linda Lear discusses an interview with one of Carson's fellow college students who said that the girls roomed together because no one else wanted to room with either of them.

Carson's classmates might not have sought her as a friend, but they respected her writing talent. Grace Croff, assistant English professor and teacher of freshman composition, also recognized Carson's fine writing skills and fostered them. Croff became a mentor to Carson. She encouraged Carson to write for the school newspaper, *The Arrow,* and for *The Englicode,* the newspaper's literary supplement.

As a freshman, Carson wrote a story for *The Englicode* called "Master of the Ship's Light." The tale contained poetic descriptions of the sea, which Carson had yet to see. She used her imagination and drew upon the many books she had read about the ocean.

Croff commented about the story, "Your style is so good because you have made what might be a relatively technical subject very intelligible to the reader." As Carson grew as a writer, similar observations about her writing were made. Carson became well known for her ability to take complicated scientific information and make it easy for the nonscientist—the everyday person—to understand.

During her freshman summer, Carson returned home. The small Carson house was crowded. Her sister, Marian, had married as a young woman, and that marriage had ended. Her second marriage had also failed, and she had moved home with her two daughters: Virginia, who was born in 1924, and Marjorie, who was born in 1925. Carson's brother, Robert; his wife, Meredith; and their baby daughter, Frances, lived in a tent in the Carson's backyard. Carson spent her summer reading and enjoying nature, and then returned to PCW for her sophomore year.

A MAJOR CHOICE

PCW required the students to take two semesters of biology. Carson enrolled in Biology 1 and 2 in her sophomore year. Her biology classes were taught by Professor Mary Scott Skinker, the acting head of the biology department. Skinker was an enthusiastic and knowledgeable teacher. She demanded excellence from her students, and they respected her.

Skinker ignited Carson's passion for biology. She found the classroom and laboratory work challenging and fascinating, but Carson most enjoyed the local field trips that Skinker organized. On these excursions, Carson and her fellow students were able to study animals and plants in their natural habitats. Skinker would quickly

Mary Scott Skinker, Rachel Carson's college biology professor, influenced her love of science and became her mentor.

become a mentor and role model to Carson. Carson also formed friendships with two science students who were a year behind her in school, Mary Frye and Dorothy Thompson.

Carson so loved biology that she debated changing her major from English to biology. PCW President Coolidge discouraged her from switching to a science major. She believed that Carson was a talented writer and saw a promising future for her as a professional writer or teacher—career paths that were open to women at the

(continues on page 40)

A MODEL TEACHER

Mary Scott Skinker was Rachel Carson's science professor at Pennsylvania College for Women in Pittsburgh, Pennsylvania. Skinker motivated Carson to pursue biology as a profession. Skinker became a friend and mentor to Carson. Their career paths went in similar directions, and each faced biases against women in science. Skinker and Carson became government scientists. They were both driven to share scientific knowledge with others— Skinker as an educator and Carson as a writer.

According to Linda Lear's description of Skinker's life in her book *Rachel Carson: Witness for Nature*, Skinker was born in Denver, Colorado, in 1891. She was the tenth of 11 children. In the early 1900s, Skinker's family moved to St. Louis, Missouri, where her father was a professional farmer.

Skinker's mother died when she was young, so her older sister Anne stepped in to raise her. When Skinker graduated from high school in 1908, she became a public school teacher.

Furthering her own education was a priority to Skinker throughout her life. In 1920, she moved back to Colorado and earned her 10-year certificate from Colorado Teachers College. Two years later, Skinker attended Columbia Teachers College in New York City and earned her bachelor's degree in science. She then received her master's degree in zoology from Columbia University.

Skinker was hired at PCW in 1923 as a faculty member and was made acting head of the biology department the following year. She was an enthusiastic and knowledgeable professor and her students respected her. However, the president of the college, Cora

Coolidge, was not an advocate of women in the sciences. Working for Coolidge became a struggle for Skinker.

Skinker had been dating the brother of PCW German professor Brunhilde Fitz-Randolph, but she opted not to commit to marriage. Instead, she left the college to pursue her Ph.D. at The Johns Hopkins University in Baltimore, Maryland.

In the summer of 1928, Skinker traveled to the Marine Biological Laboratory (MBL) in Woods Hole on Cape Cod, Massachusetts. There, she studied protozoology, the area of biology that examines single-cell organisms known as protozoa. When she returned home from her summer studies, she was in poor health and was unable to attend The Johns Hopkins University. She moved in with her sister Anne in Washington, D.C., and took doctoral classes at George Washington University. Skinker earned her Ph.D. in 1933.

At the same time, Skinker was hired to work at the Zoological Division of the U.S. Department of Agriculture's Bureau of Animal Industry as a government scientist. She was employed as a research parasitologist to study organisms that survive on or in host organisms (a field known as parasitology).

Her job went smoothly until Emmett Price became head of the division of zoology. Price did not believe that women should be scientists. For this reason, he was slow to promote women in his division. Skinker found it difficult to work for him and decided to leave government work.

Afterwards, Skinker moved around a bit. She went to New York City and became the director of a residence for women. Then she returned to teaching. She taught at Hockaday School in Dallas, Texas. Finally, she worked at National College of Education in Evanston, Illinois, where she taught others the art of teaching. Skinker died on December 19, 1948.

(continued from page 37)

time. Coolidge did not think that Carson could succeed with science as her profession because it was a male-dominated arena. Her English teacher, Croff, also encouraged Carson to continue with an English major.

One night, Carson had an enlightening experience. She sat in her dormitory room while rain pelted the windows and the wind howled outside. Carson read the poem "Locksley Hall" by Alfred, Lord Tennyson. Its final lines seemed to be created especially for her:

> Let it fall on Locksley Hall, with rain or hail, or fire or snow
> For the mighty wind arises, roaring seaward, and I go.

Carson would later write to her friend Dorothy Freeman, "I can still remember my intense emotional response as that line spoke to something within me seeming to tell me that my own path led to the sea—which then I had never seen—and that my own destiny was somehow linked with the sea."

Even though Carson's heart seemed to be leading her to choose biology as a major, her writing continued to call to her as well. Carson wrote a story for *The Englicode* called "Broken Lamps." The piece was published on May 27, 1927, and won the prestigious Omega Prize.

Carson did change her major to biology in the winter of her junior year. Both Croff and Coolidge were disappointed. Even her fellow students, who were convinced of her writing skills, gave her a hard time about the switch. Carson wrote to Mary Frye, "I've gotten bawled out and called all sorts of blankety blank names so much that it's beginning to get monotonous. That's all from the other girls, of course."

That same winter, Carson had one of her most memorable times at college. The snow had blanketed the campus, and she and a group of girls gathered sleds and borrowed trays from the cafeteria to go sledding. Afterwards, they went back to the dorms and dressed in their pajamas and robes. A fire was roaring in the drawing room fireplace and the group sang songs and ate delicious snacks. Carson also enjoyed her time playing as an alternate on the field hockey team that year. These were sweet moments of camaraderie for her.

Carson's beloved biology professor, Skinker, decided to take a leave of absence from PCW and pursue a Ph.D. in zoology at The Johns Hopkins University in Baltimore, Maryland. She would be gone for Carson's senior year. Rather than face time without her mentor, Carson planned to leave the college a year early and follow Skinker to The Johns Hopkins University. Carson was accepted to the university as a master's student, but the cost was too high for her. Instead, she stayed at PCW to complete her senior year.

Carson's last year at PCW was emotionally difficult. She missed Skinker, and she was displeased with the incompetence of Skinker's replacement. To make matters worse, Grace Croff had also chosen to leave the college.

To honor Skinker, Mary Frye and Carson founded a science club called Mu Sigma Sigma, which were Skinker's initials in Greek. Carson was the president of the club. An even greater tribute to Skinker was the earnest way Carson dedicated herself to her education. She graduated from PCW magna cum laude on June 10, 1929.

Sea Studies

Rachel Carson's lifelong love of animals coupled with her passion for science motivated her to seek her master's degree in zoology. She would attend The Johns Hopkins University in Baltimore, Maryland, beginning in the fall semester of 1929. The university awarded Carson a much-needed $200 scholarship.

The summer before starting at Johns Hopkins, Carson had the chance to go to the Marine Biological Laboratory (MBL) in Woods Hole, Massachusetts, located on the southwestern part of Cape Cod. Mary Scott Skinker had spent part of the previous summer at the MBL studying protozoa and thought it was a superb research facility. She encouraged Carson to apply for a position at the summer session. Pennsylvania College for Women chose to send Carson to the MBL and paid her admission. Carson would be responsible only for room and food costs.

After visiting at home for a bit in the summer of 1929, Carson embarked on a trip that would finally bring her to the MBL and to the ocean she had only imagined. Before her long-awaited initial view of the sea, Carson had planned a few side adventures. First,

The Johns Hopkins University, photographed in 1999, first opened in 1876. Leroy Burney, who served as the U.S. surgeon general between 1956 and 1961, was among those graduating the same year as Carson (1932). He became the first federal official to publicly identify cigarette smoking as a cause of lung cancer.

she boarded a train for Baltimore and Johns Hopkins. Carson needed to find a place to live for the fall semester because Johns Hopkins did not have dormitory rooms for women.

From Baltimore, Carson took a bus to Washington, D.C., and then traveled to Skyland, Virginia, to visit her mentor Skinker, who was staying at her family's Shenandoah Mountain cabin. The two women, now close friends, spent many hours talking. They rode horses. They hiked beneath the oak trees and marveled at the wildflowers and soaring birds. Carson and Skinker also challenged one another to multiple games of tennis.

The next stop on Carson's journey was New York City. There, she spent a day sightseeing. Carson would sail from New York City to Woods Hole on a boat. The boat trip was her first time to see the ocean. She stood on deck breathing the salt breeze and watching the waves. Carson refused to go below deck until night fell.

THE MARINE BIOLOGICAL LABORATORY

Spencer F. Baird was the first director of the Commission of Fish and Fisheries, which is now the National Marine Fisheries Service. In 1882, he set up a laboratory in Woods Hole, Massachusetts, to study marine life. Woods Hole is on the southwestern part of Cape Cod with ocean waters close at hand.

With Baird's encouragement, the Marine Biological Laboratory (MBL) was established in 1888 just across the street from his laboratory. The money to begin the MBL was raised by the Women's Association of Boston and the Boston Society of Natural History. The zoologist Charles Otis Whitman was chosen as the MBL's first director.

The purpose of the MBL was to allow biological researchers the opportunity to have hands-on experiences with marine organisms. The MBL is a private marine laboratory and is not affiliated with any university or business. For 90 years, the MBL offered only summer programs. Scientists like Rachel Carson and students like Mary Frye could come and learn from experts in the field, do research in the laboratories, and take advantage of the extensive scientific library.

As has been the case since its founding, scientists who go to the MBL have the chance to work on their experiments for long, uninterrupted periods of time. They can share ideas and discuss scientific problems with the large group of fellow scientists who also use the facility for their research. Lewis Thomas, author of *The Lives of a Cell*, described the energetic sound of the MBL scientists collaborating,

CARSON'S MARINE EXPERIENCE

Carson's time at the MBL was heavenly for her. Carson was there as a beginning investigator, surrounded by the ocean that she had longed to see. Her friend Mary Frye was at the MBL, as well, and they roomed together at a nearby boarding house. At the MBL,

"It is the most extraordinary of noises, half-shout, half-song made by confluent, simultaneously raised human voices, explaining things to each other."

At the MBL, scientists study simple sea creatures to understand complex life processes, such as the working of nerves and muscles or cell division. For example, the Woods Hole squid has unusually long nerve fibers that can be examined for insights about neurological diseases such as multiple sclerosis.

As of 2010, the MBL offers programs year-round with a staff of 274 scientists. More than 50 scientists with ties to the MBL have received Nobel Prizes in their fields.

Scientists who have worked at the MBL have made some astonishing discoveries. In the late 1980s, Mitchell Sogin, director of the MBL's Josephine Bay Paul Center for Comparative Molecular Biology and Evolution, and his colleagues found that pneumocystis, a one-celled organism that causes deadly infections in AIDS patients, is a fungus. Doctors had not realized this and are now able to look for anti-fungal medications to help these patients.

MBL researchers Joan Ruderman and Tim Hunt studied clam eggs. Early in the 1980s, they discovered a protein, which they called cyclin, that is initially found in large quantities and then disappears as cells prepare to divide and divide. In later research, Ruderman and her colleagues found that cancer cells make too much cyclin and make it at the wrong time. The cancer cells don't divide normally, and the cancer grows. Researchers are hoping that the cyclin discovery will help them to detect breast cancer in its early stage.

Before she began graduate classes at The Johns Hopkins University, Carson studied at the Marine Biological Laboratory (*seen here*) in Woods Hole, Massachusetts.

women and men worked side-by-side in the laboratories. Students researched alongside prominent scientists, some of whom had even won the Nobel Prize. No biases against women scientists seemed to exist there—scientific study was the most important focus.

Carson enjoyed wading into the ocean's tidal pools—water left behind at low tide. She would stand and examine the sea animals and plants. Other days, she went out on Vineyard Sound or to Buzzard's Bay aboard a dredging boat. The boat's fishing net would haul in fish, shells, rocks, and seaweed, which she had never seen firsthand.

In addition to studying ocean animals and plants in their natural habitat, Carson had access to large tanks filled with live sea creatures. She could also examine preserved jar specimens. At the MBL, Carson began research on what she believed would be her master's thesis topic. She planned to compare the terminal nerve of the turtle with those of the lizards and snakes.

Carson was amazed with the MBL library. It contained collections of new books with the latest scientific research and old classic scientific texts. The library also held many professional journals—magazines with articles written by scientists. In the future, Carson would return to the MBL library often to do extensive research for the books she would write.

Of course, the time at the MBL was not all work. Carson ate meals with the other MBL researchers and engaged in lively supper conversation. She picnicked on the beach with groups of friends. Frye and Carson played tennis, and Frye even tried to teach her to swim.

When Carson's time at the MBL came to an end, she headed to Washington, D.C. She had arranged a meeting with Elmer Higgins, the director of the U.S. Bureau of Fisheries, Division of Scientific Inquiry. Carson asked Higgins's advice about which courses she should take at Johns Hopkins. She also wanted his insights about job opportunities for female scientists. He was frank with Carson and said that there was much bias against women in science. He said that her best opportunity lay in becoming a science teacher or a government scientist.

In the fall of 1929, Carson began her zoology studies at Johns Hopkins. As always, she was a diligent student, doing her best in the university's challenging classes, such as genetics. That October, the stock market crash occurred, followed by the Great Depression. The Great Depression was an economic downturn that lasted 10 years. Businesses closed, and people became unemployed. Banks failed, and people lost their savings.

Carson's family suffered in the poor economy. She rented a house in Stemmers Run, on the outskirts of Baltimore, and welcomed her family to live with her. Carson's mother, father, sister Marian, and Marian's two daughters moved into her house.

It was kind of Carson to open her home to her relatives, but she also benefited from having them there. Her mother prepared meals and kept the house tidy—chores Carson disliked. This division of labor, with Carson working outside the home and her mother cooking and cleaning, would continue for the rest of their lives together.

Carson's brother Robert joined the rest of the family less than a year later. His business had not been doing well. He took a job as an estimator for a radio repair business. In those difficult economic times, people often did not have money to pay their bills. One of Robert's customers gave him a Persian cat and three kittens to partially settle a bill. Mitzi, the mother cat, and her kittens, Buzzie, Kito, and Tippy, became favorites of Carson's. From that time on, Carson was a cat lover and always kept cats as pets.

BALANCING SCHOOL AND WORK

During her first summer in Baltimore, Carson needed to find a job to help her family financially. She took a position as a teaching assistant to Grace Lippy, who taught an undergraduate zoology course at Johns Hopkins. As a teaching assistant, Carson was responsible for designing the laboratory experiments for the class. She also set up the scientific equipment for each lab, even washing every glass beaker that would be needed. Carson would give the students a hand performing the experiments as well.

Carson discovered that her second year's tuition at the university had increased. Unfortunately, her scholarship stayed the same. She could not afford to continue as a full-time student. She became a part-time graduate student and needed to find a part-time job. She was hired as a laboratory assistant at Raymond Pearl's Institute for Biological Research in the School of Hygiene and Public Health at The Johns Hopkins Medical School. At the institute, Carson helped with various experiments, including research with rats and fruit flies.

After her work there was complete, Carson was hired as a biology instructor at the Dental and Pharmacy School at the University

THE GREAT DEPRESSION

On Thursday, October 24, 1929, known as "Black Thursday," the value of stocks on the New York Stock Exchange plummeted, and billions of dollars were lost. This was the beginning of what is called the stock market crash of 1929, which lasted into mid-November of that year. By that time, an estimated $30 billion in stock value was lost.

Having shares of stock is like owning a small piece of a business. People invest in stock hoping that the business will do well

(continues)

Shantytowns—slum settlements created by impoverished people out of scrap materials—were built by homeless individuals during the Great Depression. They were popularly called Hoovervilles, after U.S. President Herbert Hoover, who some critics said allowed the country to slide into a depression. This Hooverville, pictured in September 1932, was located in New York City's Central Park.

(continued)

and that the investors will make money when they sell. Stocks were selling at all-time highs in 1928. During the crash, however, investors panicked and tried desperately to sell their shares of stock. The problem was that hardly anyone wanted to buy the stocks, and the buyers that existed were willing to pay only a low price.

The crash was followed by the Great Depression, a long, 10-year period of economic downturn. For the most part, wealthy individuals were the ones who owned stock in 1929. When they lost money, they stopped buying things. Even people who were not investors in the stock market became afraid to spend their money to make purchases.

For this reason, businesses could not sell their products, and they were forced to close. Their employees were without jobs. At the height of unemployment during the Great Depression, 13 million Americans were out of work. Farmers also suffered economic hardships.

Banks failed, and families lost their savings. Many people also lost their houses. Some built shacks and lived on the outskirts of cities. These communities of shanties were nicknamed "Hoovervilles"

of Maryland. She was the only female biology teacher at that school.

Carson juggled her school courses with her work schedule. She struggled to find a topic for her master's thesis. Her hope of studying the terminal nerves of turtles, snakes, and lizards did not pan out.

Carson finally decided to research the pronephros of the catfish. The pronephros is a temporary kidney that appears in the catfish embryo and disappears on the eleventh day, when the catfish is in the larval stage. To research the topic, she labored long hours over

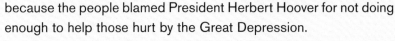

because the people blamed President Herbert Hoover for not doing enough to help those hurt by the Great Depression.

Hunger was a daily reality during the Great Depression. Many took advantage of soup kitchens and bread lines, which offered food supplied by charitable organizations. Others lived on inexpensive foods, eating mayonnaise sandwiches or tomato soup made by mixing ketchup and hot water.

In New York City, 6,000 apple vendors stood on street corners and sold apples for a nickel apiece. It was the only way they could make money to live. The economy remained poor until the start of World War II.

Today, there are U.S. government programs in place to help those in need when the economy sours. People have unemployment insurance, which supplies workers who have lost positions with some money until they can find other jobs. Money kept in U.S. banks is insured against loss by the Federal Deposit Insurance Corporation. In addition, government welfare programs give a hand to those in financial difficulty. These government safeguards are in place to make sure that Americans will not suffer as they did during the Great Depression.

the dissection table and at the microscope. She also read pages and pages of scientific journal articles. The title of Carson's completed master's thesis was, "The Development of the Pronephros during the Embryonic and Early Larval Life of the Catfish (*Ictalurus punctatus*)." With her thesis completed, Carson graduated with her master's degree in zoology on June 14, 1932.

Carson had been unable to pay the balance of her tuition at PCW. She had given the college two lots of her family's Springdale land to hold as collateral until she could pay the debt. Unfortunately, with the Great Depression and resulting poor economy, Carson was not in a position to pay the money she owed. She allowed the college to take the land as payment in the fall of 1932.

Carson continued with her education at The Johns Hopkins University in pursuit of a Ph.D. but could not afford to complete her coursework. Instead, she needed to find a full-time job. Carson left the Ph.D. program early in 1934.

The following year brought another sad event: Carson's father died on July 6, 1935. He came into the kitchen and complained of feeling unwell. He walked out the back door for some fresh air and collapsed in the backyard. The family sent his body to his sisters in Pennsylvania for burial. No one in Carson's immediate family could attend his funeral because they didn't have enough money to travel from Baltimore to the services.

Combining Science and Writing

Professor Mary Scott Skinker encouraged Rachel Carson to take some of the federal civil service exams. These would be necessary if she sought a job as a government scientist, as Skinker had. Carson scored well on the tests.

Carson made another appointment with Elmer Higgins, then division chief at the U.S. Bureau of Fisheries, to inquire about a job. Unfortunately, Higgins did not have any permanent openings.

However, Higgins's group had an assignment to write 52 radio scripts about marine life called "Romance Under the Waters"—jokingly referred to as "seven-minute fish tales" by the office personnel. His employees were struggling with writing these scripts. The scientists were having trouble translating technical information for the public.

Higgins asked Carson if she could write. Of course, her answer was "yes." He took a chance on her and let her give script writing a try. Higgins was pleased with Carson's initial scripts. She had a knack for making the scientific information understandable to and

Elmer Higgins served as the head of the Bureau of Fisheries. He hired Carson to create 52 radio segments to educate the public about marine animals and coastal water management.

enjoyable for the listening public. Higgins hired her to write the remaining scripts at $13 a week.

Later in her life, Carson would reflect on this writing work as a turning point. It allowed her to combine her two passions, science and writing. Carson told a group of female journalists, "I had given up writing forever, I thought. It never occurred to me that I was just getting something to write about."

Carson also combined her scientific knowledge with writing when she began to write freelance articles for the *Baltimore Sun* newspaper. Even these early articles demonstrated Carson's interest in conservation of natural resources and ecology, the study of the relationships between organisms and their environment. For example, she wrote an article called, "It'll be Shad-Time Soon." In this piece, Carson warned that the shad population was being threatened by water pollution and by overfishing.

In another *Baltimore Sun* article, "Fight for Wildlife Pushes Ahead," Carson called for conservation of wildlife habitats. She wrote that people were destroying animal habitats by cutting too much timber, draining marshlands, and plowing over the grasses of the prairies. The animals were losing their homes and their lives. "Wildlife . . . is dwindling because its home is being destroyed. But the home of wildlife is also our home," Carson wrote. In this article, Carson touched on a theme that would become central in her later writing—that human beings are a part of nature.

It is interesting to note that Carson suggested an article to the *Baltimore Sun* editor, Mark Watson, about how selenium and certain fluorides were contaminating the soil. She was worried that the chemicals in the soil would reach the water and harm aquatic and human life. The article topic was not used, but it showed Carson's early concern about chemicals poisoning the natural world.

When Carson's work on the radio scripts was complete, Higgins asked her to write an introduction to a U.S. Bureau of Fisheries' publication. Carson presented him with an essay called "The World of Waters." After he read the essay, Higgins gave it back to her and told her that she would have to try again. He said the piece was not right for the U.S. Bureau of Fisheries' publication. With a twinkle in his eye, Higgins suggested that Carson submit the essay to *The Atlantic Monthly,* a well-respected literary magazine. Carson was pleased by the compliment, yet she did not act on Higgins advice right away. Instead, she tucked the piece into a drawer.

On August 17, 1936, the U.S. Bureau of Fisheries hired Carson to be a full-time junior aquatic biologist, working with the Division of Scientific Inquiry with the Baltimore field office. In her new job, Carson would be studying Chesapeake Bay fish. She would also write scientific reports and publications for the public.

Tragically, Carson's sister Marian died of pneumonia in January 1937. Maria and Carson took on the responsibility of raising Marian's daughters, Virginia, 12, and Marjorie, 11. Carson moved the family to a home in Silver Spring, Maryland. The house was near good schools for the girls and it was closer to Washington, D.C., where Carson frequently traveled to do research for her job.

Carson dug her "The World of Waters" essay out of its resting place in the drawer. She made a few changes and finally sent it to *The Atlantic Monthly,* as Higgins had recommended. Edward Weeks, acting editor of the magazine, accepted the article. The newly titled piece, "Undersea," ran in the September 1937 issue.

Carson used the byline R.L. Carson for the article. She explained that she identified herself this way in government publications to avoid the bias against women scientists. About her government writings she wrote to Weeks: "We [Carson and her U.S. Bureau of Fisheries colleagues] have felt that they would be more effective . . . if they were presumably written by a man."

"Undersea" was filled with Carson's lyrical language and detailed descriptions of ocean life. For example, she wrote about the darkness of the sea depths and the exotic, glowing fish found there. She introduced her readers to the wonders of ocean animals and plants most had never imagined.

Readers were enchanted by the article. Carson received a letter from Hendrik Willem van Loon, author of *The Story of Mankind.* He praised "Undersea" enthusiastically. He said that he learned much

ON THE HOMEFRONT

When the United States entered World War II, the citizens at home pitched in to help the war effort. Rachel Carson did her part by training to become an air raid warden. Air raid wardens made sure people took precautions against air attacks, such as blocking out all the light from their houses. These "blacked out" houses could not be seen by bomber pilots at night.

Many U.S. factories stopped making their usual products and began manufacturing items needed by the military, such as uniforms, Jeeps, and tanks. Because so many men were overseas fighting, women stepped up and took their places at factories. The "Rosie the Riveter" public relations campaign encouraged women to do their part on the assembly lines. Rosie the Riveter, an American cultural icon, was portrayed as a tireless assembly worker advancing the American war effort.

Certain materials, such as steel and rubber, were needed to make goods for the military. The citizens were asked to donate scrap metal and old tires for recycling. People even collected bacon grease and other kitchen fats to donate. These were used to make explosives.

Foods were sent first to feed the fighting forces; therefore, what remained stateside was scarce. People could buy only certain amounts of these limited items, which became known as *rationing.* Citizens received ration books filled with stamps that were worth points. The red ration stamps were for items like meat and butter; the blue, for processed foods. Rationed items at the grocery stores, such as meat and sugar, were marked with prices and points. People had to pay the cashier money and ration stamps for those items.

Many households chipped in to help with the country's food production. They grew victory gardens of vegetables in their yards.

(continues)

(continued)

At their peak, victory gardens accounted for 40 percent of the vegetables produced in the United States.

Gasoline was rationed. Individuals were given a sticker with a letter of the alphabet to display in the front window of their cars. The letter indicated how many gallons of gasoline per week that person was allowed. Most people had an "A" sticker, which permitted them to buy 3 or 4 gallons a week to run errands. Workers in the military industry had "B" stickers and were allowed 8 gallons per week so that they could travel to and from work. Emergency personnel, such as firefighters and police officers, were issued a "C" sticker and could use as much gasoline as they needed. Heating oil was also rationed, depending on the size of the home and the number of children living there.

People were creative when dealing with limited goods. It was difficult to purchase silk or nylon stockings, so women began to put makeup on their legs to look like the real thing. They drew lines up the backs of their legs with eyebrow pencil to mimic the seams of seamed stockings.

The public bought war bonds to help finance the war. A person would buy a war bond for three-quarters of the bond's face value. The government used the money for military needs. When the bond reached maturity, the government paid the person back his or her initial investment plus interest.

from Carson's article and that he wanted her to share even more of her knowledge. Quincy Howe, senior editor of Simon & Schuster publishing company and van Loon's editor, also wrote to Carson. He told her that he had enjoyed the article and asked if she had thought about writing a book about the ocean. These complimentary letters spurred Carson to consider just such a project.

Women became an integral part of the workforce during World War II, when many men were out of the county fighting the war. In this image, three women assemble aircraft gun turrets by hand.

Many women helped the United Service Organizations (USO) entertain military members. These women would act as hostesses at social events. They served doughnuts to the service members and danced and chatted with them, which made the soldiers feel appreciated.

UNDER THE SEA WIND

In January 1938, Carson met with van Loon, his wife, and Howe at the van Loon home in Old Greenwich, Connecticut. Howe expressed an interest in having Carson write a book about the sea, which he could publish. Before he offered her a publishing contract, he wished to have her submit an outline and a sample chapter.

Because Carson was working full time and writing newspaper articles, it took a long time for her to complete the promised outline and chapter. She sent the outline of the book to Howe by June of 1939 and five chapters in the spring of 1940. Howe finalized a contract with Carson in June of that year.

All told, Carson worked for three years on her book *Under the Sea Wind*. She wrote at night after long workdays. She needed to be alone in the quiet to do her best writing. Carson would close herself in her bedroom with only her cats, Buzzie and Kito, for company.

Carson wrote longhand and constantly revised as she went. She would rearrange words and sentences. Often, she changed words to more precise or descriptive ones. Carson would read sections aloud to make certain she liked the sound of the words. She wanted to be sure that the words flowed well and that the meaning was clear. Sometimes, she even had her mother, Maria, read portions of the manuscripts out loud to her. Finally, Maria typed all the chapters.

At last, Carson finished the manuscript and submitted it to Howe. *Under the Sea Wind* was published on November 1, 1941. In the book, Carson tells the story of the lives of three sea animals. She writes of their struggle to find food, to survive predators, and to breed. The book is filled with poetic descriptions of the animals' habitats. The tales are told from each animal's point of view. Carson worked hard to keep the human perspective absent from the story.

People are mentioned in the book as fishermen. Carson portrays them as natural predators to the animals. In their nets, the fishermen catch some fish that are too small to eat and that are thoughtlessly discarded on the beach. However, the dead fish are not wasted because birds and crabs eat them.

In his book *The Gentle Subversive*, Mark Hamilton Lytle uses the discarded fish passage as an example of Carson's optimistic view of the natural world. She presents the harsh realities of death in nature but also celebrates nature's cycle of continuation. Carson writes, "For in the sea, nothing is lost. One dies, another lives, as the precious elements of life are passed on and on in endless chains."

BATS AND ECHOLOCATION

Bats are flying mammals. They are nocturnal, which means they are active at night. Still, they manage to travel safely and hunt in the dark.

Small bats, whose scientific name is *microchiroptera,* have small eyes and big ears. These bats use echolocation to fly around in the dark without bumping into objects. They also use echolocation to hunt and capture prey. For the most part, small bats search for insects to eat.

Echolocation means the bat uses sound wave echoes to find objects. The bat sends out vocal sounds from its mouth or nose. The sound waves from those cries hit objects, bounce off, and echo back to the bat. The bat is equipped with large ears and a spike of cartilage in each ear called a tragus. The ear and tragus help gather the echoed sound. The bat's brain is able to take information from the echoes and translate them.

Echolocation can tell a bat how far an object is from the bat. The faster the echoes return to the bat, the closer the object. Far-away objects take longer to bounce the echo back toward the bat. Echolocation can also help the bat determine an object's shape and texture. Amazingly, echolocation allows a bat to avoid an obstacle as small as the width of a human hair.

Echolocation can also let the bat know an object's size. The smaller the item, the fewer sound waves echo back. The larger objects send more echoes back to the bat. A bat can even figure out which direction an insect is flying. If the echo reaches the bat's left ear first and then the right, the insect is moving from the bat's left side to its right side.

Bats' echolocation cries are ultrasonic and are too high frequency to be heard by humans. Bats send out cries less frequently when they are just flying around than when they have located prey. Red bats, for example, sent out echolocation cries of about 10–20 per second

(continues)

(continued)

when they are merely flying. They increase their cries to 200 sounds per second when they locate prey and need to home in on it.

Bats that hunt in open areas use louder cries to echolocate. They need to be louder for the sound to reach the objects, which are farther away from them in these open spaces. These bats are called "shouters." On the other hand, bats that hunt in wooded areas use quieter cries and are known as "whisperers."

Bats' ability to echolocate is millions of times more efficient than radar technology. Radar is short for *radio detection and ranging* because radar uses radio waves to judge the distance and location of objects similarly to how the bat uses sound waves. Rachel Carson wrote the article "The Bat Knew It First" for *Collier's* magazine in 1944 to explain the similarity of bat echolocation to radar.

By the way, it is not surprising that Carson appreciated bats because they control the insect population naturally. A small bat uses echolocation to eat thousands of mosquito-sized insects every night. In many species of small bats, a pregnant female can consume her body weight in insects each night. Bats help control pests that eat crops and that carry diseases. They reduce the need for man-made pesticide use.

In addition, large bats, whose scientific name is *megachiroptera,* feed on flowers and fruit. They pollinate plants and spread

The first character in *Under the Sea Wind* is a sanderling named Silverbar. Carson follows Silverbar from Patagonia, an area in southern South America, to its breeding grounds in the Arctic. She describes the challenges the sanderling faces when trying to find food. She also writes about the bird's struggle to keep its young safe from predators.

Scomber the mackerel is the next animal Carson introduces. As an egg, Scomber floats on the ocean surface. There, he is vulnerable

Rachel Carson wrote a 1944 magazine article to help people understand how bat echolocation worked like radar. In part because Carson had a natural affinity for animals, she enjoyed helping others understand their unique, complex ways of life.

seeds. Ninety-five percent of the rain forest's new growth is attributable to these bats. Carson would have loved the fact that large bats are so effective at replenishing natural resources.

to predators such as comb jellies. As a young mackerel, Scomber still has to fight for his life from the threat posed by dogfish and fishermen.

Lastly, Carson presents Anguilla the eel. Anguilla is born in the depths of the Sargasso Sea. The Sargasso Sea is an area of the Atlantic Ocean south of Bermuda. The eel travels long distances to the freshwater streams to live for many years. Then,

Anguilla undertakes the amazing journey back to the Sargasso Sea to breed.

Many magazines and newspapers, such as *The New Yorker* and *The New York Times,* published positive critiques of *Under the Sea Wind.* Book reviewers praised Carson's beautiful language and scientific accuracy. The famous oceanographer, William Beebe, also wrote a flattering review for *The Saturday Review of Literature.* He liked the book so much that he asked to include two of its chapters in a nature anthology he was compiling.

Unfortunately, just one month after *Under the Sea Wind* was published, the Japanese attacked the U.S. Naval Base at Pearl Harbor. The United States quickly declared war on Japan. At that point, the American people were focused on the war effort and were not interested in reading a book about the sea. Fewer than 2,000 copies of Carson's first book were sold.

Carson put the disappointing sales of her first book behind her. In May 1942, she was promoted to assistant aquatic biologist for the U.S. Fish and Wildlife Service (FWS). The U.S. Bureau of Fisheries had been reorganized and renamed in July 1939.

Another change was coming for Carson. Those government officials who were directly involved in the war effort needed office space. For this reason, Carson would be relocated to Chicago. Carson and her mother made the move, but Virginia and Marjorie were old enough not to have to go with them and it is believed that they stayed behind in Silver Spring with friends.

During World War II, many items were rationed. This meant that certain goods, such as meat and gasoline, were scarce, and people could buy only a limited quantity of those items. Carson produced a series of FWS publications called, "Food from the Sea." These bulletins included various types of seafood, which would make delicious substitutions for rationed meat. In the publications, Carson described the habitats and life cycles of the sea creatures. She also offered nutritional information and recipes. Carson hoped the publications would entice people to try different fish and shellfish instead of the more familiar, overfished varieties.

Less than one year later, Carson was moved back to her office in Washington, D.C. She was promoted to associate aquatic biologist and, just six months later, to aquatic biologist. In all her positions at the FWS, Carson's work involved scientific writing and editing rather than work in the laboratory.

Much new scientific information related to the war crossed Carson's desk. She was able to use this as research for her freelance writing. Carson wrote an article comparing bats' ability to echolocate and the military's radar technology. The resulting article, "The Bat Knew It First," was published in *Collier's* magazine and was reprinted in the *Reader's Digest*. It was even placed in U.S. Navy recruiting offices across the country to clearly explain radar.

Carson became restless with her government job and sought another position. The timing wasn't right for a job search, however. Men were returning from war duty, and they were given any available work. Carson tried unsuccessfully for an editorial position at the *Reader's Digest*. All of the editors at that magazine were men.

Carson contacted naturalist William Beebe at the New York Zoological Society, but he said that only low-level positions were available. She also tried to find work with the National Audubon Society without success. Finally, Carson stayed in her position at the FWS.

Diving into the Sea

Working at the U.S. Fish and Wildlife Service (FWS) was fortunate for Rachel Carson. She took part in conferences with ocean experts and saw many military reports about the sea. She could use these resources as research for her next book.

The crews of ships and submarines on sea duty during World War II discovered more about ocean tides, currents, and the land-scape of the ocean floor. The reports on these new findings often crossed Carson's desk. She also learned about new technology, like radar, which she had used for the *Collier's* magazine bat echoloca-tion article.

One of the discoveries that caught Carson's attention was the insecticide dichlorodiphenyltrichloroethane, or DDT. DDT was first made in 1874 by an Austrian chemist, Othmar Zeidler. In 1939, Swiss chemist Paul Muller realized that DDT was effective in kill-ing insects. During World War II, the U.S. military dusted DDT directly on service members to destroy lice. Lice carried the bac-teria that caused typhus. In 1943, Naples, Italy, suffered a typhus epidemic, and DDT was used to kill the lice and stop the disease.

For those fighting in the Pacific region, mosquito-borne illnesses, such as malaria, were a problem. DDT was successfully used to kill the mosquitoes. Muller was awarded the Nobel Prize in 1948 for his contribution.

After the war, the U.S. government allowed the DuPont company to sell DDT to the general public as an insecticide. However, some scientists were worried about the harmful effects of DDT on wildlife. Elmer Higgins and wildlife biologist Clarence Cottam were two such scientists. They wrote reports examining the effects of DDT on animals. Carson read their findings.

Carson became concerned about the negative effects of DDT, and on July 15, 1945, she proposed an article on this topic to *Reader's Digest* magazine. Carson told the editors that Patuxent Research Refuge, nearby to her Maryland home, was investigating how DDT affected wildlife. She could use their scientists as resources for the article. *Reader's Digest* did not wish to publish the piece because the editors of the magazine were not willing to examine the possible negative effects of chemicals. At that time, the country saw chemical advancements in a positive light, and *Reader's Digest* reflected that view.

PROTECTING WILDLIFE

In answer to a "Women in Government" survey, Carson described the work she was doing at the FWS: "It is really just the work of a small publishing house." Carson had six people working for her. She researched, wrote, and edited publications. She was also responsible for details, such as choosing artwork and typeface.

Carson made two close friends through her job, FWS artists Katherine Howe and Shirley Briggs. They spent fun times together during and after work hours. Carson and Briggs shared a love of bird watching and participated in trips organized by the Washington, D.C. Audubon Society. For example, they visited Hawk Mountain Sanctuary in Pennsylvania. There, Carson and Briggs braved the chilly weather to watch hawks with majestic wingspans soar and glide.

Carson decided to produce 12 government publications high-lighting the National Wildlife Refuges. The series was called, "Conservation in Action." She wanted to let the American people know about the importance of wildlife refuges. Wildlife refuges are lands acquired by the government as protected habitats for animals. People were building and, in the process, destroying wildlife living spaces, so wildlife refuges gave these animals a safe place to live.

The refuges were, and still are, actively managed to make sure that animals in the refuges have plenty of their natural food. For example, the waterfowl refuge park rangers often lower the water level in the refuges. This allows the plants that the birds need for food to grow. Then, the water level is raised again because the birds like to eat in a wet environment. The rangers also eliminate invasive plant species and brush, which are crowding out the animals' food. In addition, they protect endangered species from being disturbed. One example of this is that the rangers make sure there is adequate plant cover for the animals to raise their young in safety.

Carson would write four—and co-write another—of the "Conservation in Action" publications. They would describe the wildlife refuges in Virginia, Massachusetts, North Carolina, Utah, and Montana. She planned to visit each refuge as research.

Carson and Briggs began with a trip in April 1946. They visited Chincoteague National Wildlife Refuge in Virginia, which is located mostly on Assateague Island. Chincoteague is a waterfowl refuge with a large concentration of greater snow geese and black ducks. The refuge also had shorebirds that Carson was happy to observe, such as sandpipers and black skimmers.

In September 1946, Carson went to the Parker River National Wildlife Refuge in Massachusetts with Katherine Howe. Parker River had an abundance of waterfowl and shorebirds. After the refuge visit, Carson took a side trip to see Dr. Henry Bigelow, who had been the director of Woods Hole Oceanographic Institution and was then the oceanographic curator at the Museum of Comparative Zoology at Harvard University. Carson wanted to know about his current ocean research. Bigelow suggested that she write a book

Dr. Henry Bigelow (*right*), along with Harvard Professor Thomas Barbour (*center*) and artist Myvanny Dick (*left*), examines an unknown species of deep-sea fish in 1943. Bigelow encouraged Carson to write about the ocean.

about the sea for the everyday person. This idea would blossom into Carson's next book.

Next, Carson and Howe traveled to Mattamuskeet National Wildlife Refuge in North Carolina. This refuge also specialized in waterfowl and had Canada geese, snow geese, and whistling swans. Carson was especially drawn to the swans. She wrote, "The name 'whistling swan' is given because of a single high note sometimes uttered—a sound that suggests a woodwind instrument in its quality."

Finally, Carson and Howe made the long journey to refuges in Montana and Utah and to observe FWS activities in Oregon. This trip was exciting because they were able to see the animals and fish of the northwest, such as bison and salmon, respectively.

Since the financial disappointment of her first book, Carson had concentrated on writing magazine articles. Charles Alldredge, a former colleague of Carson's, recommended she find a literary agent. He supplied her with a list of possible agents. Literary agents help a writer sell his or her work to publishers and are then paid a certain percentage of the writer's earnings.

Carson was reluctant to share her earnings with an agent because her finances were tight. She finally decided to meet with literary agent Marie Rodell. In addition to being an agent, Rodell was a writer of mystery novels. She had also been a book editor at a publishing company. Carson liked Rodell and chose to hire her as an agent.

Rodell was a hard-working and knowledgeable agent. She believed in Carson's writing talent and worked long hours to make sure that Carson's writing was published and reached the public. Carson appreciated Rodell as a professional and grew to consider her a trusted friend.

As Carson began one close friendship, another was ending. Carson received word that her mentor and longtime friend, Mary Scott Skinker, was dying of cancer. She flew to Chicago to be by her hospital bedside. Skinker died a month later on December 19, 1948. Carson's feelings of loss were so deep that she kept them to herself.

Carson decided that Dr. Bigelow's idea about an ocean book was a good one. She chose to write a book about the wonders of the ocean. Carson wished she could take time off from her job and concentrate only on her research and writing. William Beebe, the oceanographer and explorer, wrote Carson a recommendation for the Eugene F. Saxton Memorial Fellowship Grant from Harper & Brothers publishing company. Carson was awarded the $2,250 fellowship, which allowed her the financial freedom to take a leave of absence from FWS.

Philip Vaudrin was editor of Oxford University Press. He was interested in seeing an outline and sample chapters of Carson's new book. Rodell sent the samples his way, and the book contract was signed on June 28, 1949.

HANDS-ON RESEARCH

As research for Carson's book, Beebe had strongly suggested that she make an undersea dive. He believed that observing ocean life from diving depths would enrich her ocean book. He recommended his favorite diving location, Bermuda, but Carson could not afford the trip. Instead, she made her dive off the coast of Florida.

There, Carson donned an 84-pound (38.1-kilogram) diving helmet and climbed down the boat's ladder below the ocean's surface. The weather was stormy, and the currents were so strong that she was unable to leave the ladder. The water was cloudy. Even so, Carson felt the experience of being under the ocean and sharing the habitat of the sea creatures was worthwhile.

She wrote to Beebe about her dive, "The difference between having dived—even under those conditions—and never having dived is so tremendous that it formed one of those milestones of life, after which everything seems a little different."

Later that summer, Carson took another journey that would help her write her book. Carson wanted to board the FWS vessel, the *Albatross III.* The *Albatross III* was going to Georges Bank, 200 miles (321.86 km) east of Boston, Massachusetts, to investigate a decline in the commercial fish there. At first, the FWS officials were reluctant to let a single woman make the trip with the all-male crew. Marie Rodell offered to go along, so the officials agreed.

The ship's crew was not welcoming to the women. The men made sure to tell Carson and Rodell horrible tales about what could happen on the vessel—tales of broken bones and seasickness. Yet the women were not frightened by the stories. They were determined to travel on the ship.

At night, deafening bumps and scraping woke Carson and Rodell. They realized it was the fishing net gathering sea creatures.

In the morning, the crew laughed and asked how the women had slept. Rodell joked that they thought they heard a mouse, but went right back to sleep. That stopped the men's teasing.

Carson was excited to see the unusual marine life that the ship's fishing nets dumped on the deck. She viewed creatures she had never seen before. She saw deep-sea starfish, heart urchins, and "such odd beings as sea mice."

Carson also watched sharks swimming near the boat. But then the crew did something that disturbed her a great deal. "There was something very beautiful about those sharks to me—and when

Dr. William Beebe (*center*) stands by his bathysphere with two assistants in this 1932 image.

WILLIAM BEEBE: OCEAN EXPLORER

Charles William Beebe was a bird expert, as well as an oceanographer, explorer, and author. Beebe was born on July 29, 1877, in Brooklyn, New York, but spent much of his childhood in East Orange, New Jersey. As a boy, he was fascinated by nature. He used to examine bugs in his backyard and raise chickens. He had his first magazine article published in January 1895 in *Harper's Young People.* The piece was about the brown creeper, a small bird.

Beebe attended Columbia University in New York City. He was one course away from earning his degree when an irresistible job opportunity came his way. He was hired to work for the New York Zoological Society at its newly opened Bronx Zoological Park. Beebe was the zoo's assistant curator of birds. He cared for the birds in the zoo's collection. He was also responsible for breeding the birds and helping to rear the young so the collection would expand. Beebe proved so skilled at his job that he would be promoted to curator of birds.

Beginning in 1903, Beebe traveled to locations all over the world, including Mexico, Trinidad, British Guiana, and China. He was collecting bird specimens and other exotic animals for the zoo. Beebe wrote books about his travels. All told, he had 24 books published during his lifetime.

In 1908, Beebe met President Theodore Roosevelt. Roosevelt had admired one of Beebe's books and invited him to the White House. They shared an interest in nature conservation. During his presidency, Roosevelt had the federal government protect 230 million acres (93 million hectares) of land. For example, he designated 150 national forests and 51 federal bird reservations. Considering their mutual respect for nature, it is not surprising that Roosevelt and Beebe became good friends.

(continues)

(continued)

In 1923, the zoo made Beebe director of its Department of Tropical Research. On one of his trips to the Galapagos Islands, he made his first undersea dive. Beebe donned a diving helmet. At that time, divers didn't have oxygen tanks, so air was pumped into the helmet through a hose. As he descended below the ocean's surface, he felt pain in his ears caused by the pressure change. He swallowed hard to equalize the pressure. Beebe was enchanted by the living creatures he observed around the coral reef, such as colorful parrot fish and crabs.

Beebe longed to dive deeper into the ocean, but a diver could go only so deep with a diving helmet and hose. Otis Barton, an engineer, approached Beebe with his idea for a deep-sea diving vessel called the bathysphere. The spherical shape of the vessel would distribute the ocean's pressure evenly across the bathysphere's surface. Beebe believed the bathysphere would work effectively for deep ocean dives.

The bathysphere, which was made of steel, weighed 5,400 pounds (2,449 kg) and had walls that were 1.5 inches (3.81 centimeters) thick. It was lowered from a ship into the ocean by a

some of those men got out their rifles and killed them for 'sport,' it really hurt me," she later reflected. This was an indication of Carson's concern about animal welfare, a cause that she would pursue in the future.

On board the *Albatross III,* Carson experienced the ocean currents and watched the sea fog settling around the boat. She would be able to use many of these moments in the book she was writing.

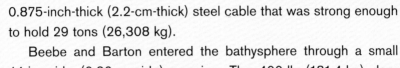

0.875-inch-thick (2.2-cm-thick) steel cable that was strong enough to hold 29 tons (26,308 kg).

Beebe and Barton entered the bathysphere through a small 14-in.-wide (0.36-m-wide) opening. The 400-lb (181.4-kg) door was then closed and secured with 10 bolts. A rubber hose attached to the sphere contained electric and telephone lines.

The dives in the bathysphere were dangerous. If the cable broke, the men would be lost in the ocean. If the sphere were crushed by the pressure of the water, they would die. But Beebe's need to explore outweighed the dangers.

The men did three years of practice dives in the Bermuda area. On August 15, 1934, the men performed their record-breaking dive off Nonsuch Island near Bermuda. Beebe and Barton descended 3,028 ft (923 m). It took two hours to go down and another hour to come back to the surface. In the ocean depths, Beebe saw amazing creatures that no one else had ever seen. No wonder he encouraged Rachel Carson to make an ocean dive.

After his deep ocean dive, Beebe left future dives to others. He returned to his tropical research for the zoo and established the New York Zoological Tropical Research Station in Trinidad. Beebe retired at age 75 from his long, illustrious career. He died June 4, 1962.

THE SEA AROUND US

Before Carson's book *The Sea Around Us* was published, *The Yale Review* included one of the chapters, "The Birth of an Island," in its magazine. Carson was paid only $75 for the piece, but she knew it would be eligible for the $1,000 American Association for the Advancement of Science Westinghouse Award. She did indeed win this award on December 8, 1950.

William Shawn, the editor of *The New Yorker* chose to use nine chapters of *The Sea Around Us* for the magazine. He paid Carson $7,500. Shawn condensed the chapters into three parts. These would be published before *The Sea Around Us* to tempt readers to buy the entire book. The first installment was published on June 2, 1951. *The New Yorker* received more letters about Carson's piece than the magazine had ever gotten before.

Oxford and Rodell made sure that advanced copies of the book went to influential people who could help sell the book by word of mouth. One of these people was Alice Roosevelt Longworth, the daughter of President Theodore Roosevelt. Longworth telephoned to let Carson know how much she had loved the book—she said she had stayed up all night reading it.

The Sea Around Us was published on July 2, 1951, by Oxford University Press. In the book, Carson makes complex concepts about currents, tides, waves, and the landscape of the ocean floor understandable to the everyday person. Her descriptions of the ocean and its creatures are vivid and poetic.

In *The Sea Around Us*, Carson discusses the ocean's beginnings. She explains how sea creatures evolved to become land dwellers. One of Carson's strong beliefs was that human beings are interconnected with nature. To make that point, she writes that human infants in the uterus evolve "from gill-breathing inhabitants of a water world to creatures able to live on land," just as the early sea creatures did.

Carson describes the dark depths of the ocean in one portion of the book. Sunlight doesn't reach much lower than 600 feet (183 meters) below the ocean's surface. Plants cannot exist without the sun's rays, so they do not live at these depths. Without plants to eat, some animals live by ingesting particles of dead matter that fall from the upper ocean layers. Other animals prey on their fellow creatures in the deep.

The animals in the deep ocean adapt to the lack of light. Some have large eyes with more rods, which are special light-sensing cells that allow these animals to see in low light. Others are totally blind. Many of the creatures of the deep are bioluminescent. They produce their own light and glow.

Carson also dispels the myth that the ocean depths are quiet. She says that the snapping of shrimp claws and the noises of croaker fish can be heard in the deep sea.

In another chapter, Carson discusses ocean islands and their native plants and animals. She writes that most ocean islands are formed through volcanic eruption. The life that begins on these islands is often unique to that island and cannot be found anywhere else.

Carson highlights the negative effects man has had on ocean islands. "But man, unhappily, has written one of his blackest records as destroyer of the ocean's island," she writes. "He has seldom set foot on an island that he has not brought about disastrous changes." Humans harming nature becomes a central theme in Carson's future writing.

Carson writes about a shipwreck on Lord Howe Island. The rats that were aboard the ship invaded the island. They killed the entire population of several native species of birds, such as the Lord Howe starling.

Carson also discusses Captain Makee, who added a decorative plant called pamakani to his garden on the Hawaiian Island of Maui. The plant was not native to Maui and was invasive. The seeds blew to every Hawaiian Island, and the pamakani crowded out native plants.

The Sea Around Us is filled with Carson's beautiful word choices and colorful images. She writes about the sunset on her journey aboard the *Albatross III*: "Evenings, the sun, before it set, was a pale silver disc hung in the ship's rigging." She also writes this poetic passage about the sea currents meshing the oceans' waters:

> The surf that we find exhilarating at Virginia Beach or at La Jolla today may have lapped at the base of Antarctic icebergs or sparkled in the Mediterranean sun, years ago, before it moved through dark unseen waterways to the place we find it now. It is by the deep, hidden currents that oceans are made one.

(continues on page 80)

ADAPTING TO OCEAN DEPTHS

Creatures that live in the ocean depths had to adapt to their harsh, dark environment. They do not live in sunshine. The sun's rays don't reach much deeper than 600 feet (183 m) into the ocean. In this dark area of the sea, no plants grow. The animals there live on particles of dead creatures and plants that fall from the upper ocean layers. Of course, they also prey on one another.

Because there is little food available in the deep, some fish, such as the deep sea angler, have teeth that slant inward. This makes it difficult for prey to escape from the angler's mouth. Other creatures are jawless or have hinged jaws so they can eat as big a meal as possible when prey is available. For the same reason, some deep-sea animals have expandable stomachs.

Deep-sea life is under intense pressure from the water around them. To survive this pressure, the animals have adapted. Many are jelly-like and have few or flexible bones.

How do these animals function in the dark? Some of them have larger eyes with more rods, which are light-sensing cells, so they can see in little light.

Many creatures of the deep are bioluminescent. Bioluminescence is a chemical process that allows an organism to make its own light. In other words, the animals glow. Dr. Edith Widder, Ocean Research & Conservation Association founder and senior scientist, is an expert in bioluminescence. She says that being surrounded by these glowing animals is "like being in the middle of a fireworks display."

Many animals use bioluminescence to attract mates and to lure prey. Widder discovered that an octopus species called *Stauroteuthis syrtensis* has bioluminescent organs called photophores in place of the suckers on its arms. The octopus uses the lights to attract a mate in the dark environment. The light also attracts its prey, tiny sea animals called copepods. The viperfish has a dorsal fin tipped with a bioluminescent photophore to attract prey.

Bioluminescent animals light up brightly when they are in danger from predators. This helps them attract bigger animals that may attack the predator that is chasing them. This is a last ditch effort to escape.

Some of the creatures even use bioluminescence as a way to camouflage themselves so predators won't see them. For example, the plainfin midshipman has lights on its underside to match any sunlight from the ocean's surface. This helps it blend into the environment and makes it harder for predators below to notice it. This phenomenon is known as counterillumination.

Bioluminescence is the production and emission of light from a living organism. This slender lantern shark, a deep-water dweller that is found is Tasmania, Australia, has bioluminescent organs. Their glow can be seen in the dark trenches of the ocean floor.

(*continued from page 77*)

ACCLAIM

Carson had been worried that the Korean War would affect book sales of *The Sea Around Us* in the way that World War II had affected her first book. She needn't have been concerned. As soon as *The Sea Around Us* was on bookstore shelves, it was a hit. The book stayed on *The New York Times* Best Seller List for 86 weeks.

Carson was presented with the prestigious National Book Award for nonfiction for *The Sea Around Us* on January 27, 1952. She also won the John Burroughs Medal for a nature book of literary merit on April 7, 1952. *The Sea Around Us* was chosen as an alternate selection by the Book-of-the-Month Club, which would bring additional money Carson's way.

Carson received piles of complimentary letters about the book. Many of the letter writers said that the book offered relief from present-day worries. The book gave such a long-term perspective of the ocean and its inhabitants that it made everyday difficulties seem less important.

Some of the fan letters offered challenges. James Bennet, a New York attorney, thought that Carson must not believe in God because she wrote about evolution. Carson told him that a belief in God and in evolution could exist together. She wrote that evolution is "a method by which God created and is still creating life on Earth."

Other letters reflected a bias against women. One man addressed his letter to Miss Carson, but began the letter with "Dear Sir." "He explained his salutation by saying that he had always been convinced that the males possess the supreme intellectual power of the world and he could not bring himself to reverse his convictions," noted Carson.

With the success of the book, Carson was called upon to make public appearances and speeches, but she was not comfortable in this role. Carson was a very private person. For *Rachel Carson: Witness for Nature*, Linda Lear interviewed Ruth Swisshelm, one of Carson's former college classmates. Swisshelm said Carson told her

Rachel Carson (*second from right*) stands with two other winners of the National Book Award, presented in 1952. From left to right are Marianne Moore, author of *Collected Poems of Marianne Moore;* James Jones, author of *From Here to Eternity;* and John Mason Brown, author and toastmaster for the ceremony.

that "she was much happier going barefoot in the sand than she was standing on a hardwood floor in high heels."

Carson was facing a difficult time in her personal life at the same time that the book was experiencing wonderful success. Her unmarried niece Marjorie became pregnant. In the 1950s, this was scandalous. Carson fought hard to keep the news private for Marjorie's sake and for her own. She would later reflect on this stressful time in a letter to her friend Dorothy Freeman. "All that followed the publication of *The Sea*—the acclaim, the excitement on the part of the critics and the public at discovering a 'promising' new writer—was simply blotted out for me by the private tragedy that engulfed me at precisely that time," she wrote. "I know it will never happen again and, if I am ever bitter, it is about that."

Poisoning Ourselves

Rachel Carson's niece Marjorie gave birth to a son, Roger Chris- tie, on February 18, 1952. Carson did not yet know what a vital role she would play in her grandnephew's life.

The success of *The Sea Around Us* gave Carson freedom from financial worry. She also had her first book, *Under the Sea Wind*, published anew by Oxford University Press, and it did well. Conse- quently, Carson was able to resign from the U.S. Fish and Wildlife Service; her resignation took effect June 3, 1952. Free from her FWS work obligations, she could devote herself more fully to her writing.

Carson had been awarded the Guggenheim Fellowship for the work on her proposed next book about the ecology of the Atlantic coast. Because of her newfound prosperity, she no longer needed the fellowship money. She chose to give some of the money back, so someone else could benefit.

Carson and her mother had vacationed in Maine during the summer of 1946. She had fallen in love with the area and confided to Shirley Briggs that she hoped to own a home there someday.

Rachel Carson sits in front of her typewriter in January 1952.

In September 1952, Carson bought her dream property in West Southport Island, Maine.

The land was wooded and overlooked the Sheepscot River. Sometimes, Carson saw seals and even whales. She had a cottage built that had a study for her books and microscope. Carson would go down to the tidal pools and gather sea animals and plants to study under the microscope. Then, she would return them to their natural habitat—just as her mother had taught her to do as a child. She would take walks in her woods to admire the birds, as well.

A TREASURED FRIENDSHIP

Soon after she bought the Maine property, Carson received a welcome letter from her new neighbor, Dorothy Freeman. Dorothy and her husband, Stanley, were excited to have Carson move nearby. They were great fans of *The Sea Around Us.*

Carson and Maria met the Freemans in person when they moved into the cottage in July 1953. Carson and Dorothy quickly became the best of friends. They had lots in common. They both loved the sea, nature, writing, and cats. Each woman was caring for an elderly mother and understood its challenges.

Dorothy enjoyed writing. She kept a daily diary and wrote faithfully to many friends. Dorothy and Carson began writing letters to one another and continued until Carson's death—for more than a decade. Of their letters, 750 remain.

These letters give insight into Carson's innermost thoughts and feelings. Carson and Dorothy wrote about everything from writing and wildlife to music and eternity. The letters were very loving, filled with many expressions of deep friendship.

Sometimes the letters were in two parts. One part was meant to be shared with the family; the other was to be read privately. The women called these private letters "apples." Carson and Dorothy also had a tradition of sending a special note to be read alone on Christmas Eve. Certain letters were destroyed because Carson did not want them made public.

In one of her letters to Dorothy, Carson shared a charming story that showed how much she cared about living things. Carson and Marjorie had gone down to the Maine beach at night. They watched as glowing sea creatures, probably single-celled bioluminescent organisms known as dinoflagellates, floated on the waves. All of a sudden, a firefly dove into the sea, maybe mistaking the

Dorothy Freeman, a close friend of Carson's in Maine, shared Carson's love of nature. Together, they worried about the over-development of local land and planned to save a beloved tract of forest next to Carson's property.

sea creatures for one of its own kind. Carson rescued the firefly in a bucket, let its wings dry, and released if far from the dangers of the ocean.

In another letter, Carson shared her disappointment with the RKO movie *The Sea Around Us.* Carson had signed a contract with

RKO to make the film based on her book. Unfortunately, Marie Rodell didn't have much experience with movie contracts. The agreement did not allow Carson to make final changes in the movie script; therefore, the film contained scientific mistakes that Carson was unable to correct. She was not happy with the movie. Even so, the movie version of *The Sea Around Us* won the 1953 Academy Award for the best full-length documentary.

EXPLORING THE SEASHORE

Before *The Sea Around Us* was published, Paul Brooks, editor-in-chief of Houghton Mifflin's general book department, approached Carson about writing a guide to the seashore. This would be Carson's next book.

Brooks's editor, Rosalind Wilson, had given him the idea for the seashore guide. Her family owned a home on Cape Cod in Massachusetts. They had some guests visiting at the shore house. The visitors took a walk along the beach and saw "stranded" horseshoe crabs. They "rescued" the crabs by throwing them back into the ocean. The guests didn't realize that the horseshoe crabs were breeding and laying eggs. Wilson said a seashore guide was needed to prevent this type of mistake.

To research her seashore guide, *The Edge of the Sea*, Carson traveled from the rocky shores of Maine to the sandy beaches of the Carolinas to the coral reefs of the Florida Keys. She spent time at the MBL on Cape Cod, as well. Carson knew that she could interview many science experts at the MBL in the summer, which would save her the trouble of finding those scientists throughout the country at other times of the year. She recommended her colleague and friend Bob Hines, an artist with the FWS, as illustrator for the book.

The Edge of the Sea was serialized in *The New Yorker* beginning August 20, 1955. The book was published by Houghton Mifflin in October 1955. It would climb to Number 3 on *The New York Times* Best Seller List.

In *The Edge of the Sea,* Carson describes three different sea-shore environments: the rock coast, the sand beach, and the coral reefs. She paints memorable pictures of each with the written word.

When discussing the shore environments, Carson gives detailed descriptions of the sea creatures and plants specific to that area. For example, the rocky coast has animals and plants that cling to or hide beneath rocks, including barnacles and periwinkles. In the chapters about the sand beach, Carson writes about creatures such as the poisonous Portuguese man-of-war. On the coral reef, Carson says that there are sponges that welcome snapping shrimp to live inside them. The sponge provides shelter to the shrimp, and they give the sponge some protection from predators.

After the publication of her book, Carson was asked to write a script for the Omnibus television series on CBS. The subject was clouds. She wrote all about low-flying stratus clouds; beautiful, fluffy cumulous clouds; and high-flying cirrus clouds made of small ice particles. Carson didn't own a television set, so she watched the program at her brother's house. It aired on May 11, 1956. She was so impressed with the final product that she went out and bought her own TV set.

Woman's Home Companion magazine asked Carson to write an article that had a personal touch. She wrote the article "Help Your Child to Wonder" to teach adults how to help children appreciate the natural world. The article described the way she and her grand-nephew Roger walked outside together and marveled at wildlife, such as tree seedlings and insects. Carson didn't think adults should force children to memorize nature facts. Instead, she believed adults could help children use all their senses to explore nature. She wanted them to have fun discovering wildlife together. Carson felt that these moments would result in children having a lifelong love of wildlife. After Carson's death, this article would be published as a book and titled *The Sense of Wonder.*

Tragically, Carson's niece Marjorie died of pneumonia on January 30, 1957. She was 31 years old. She left behind Roger, who was only five years old. Carson chose to adopt him.

SILENT SPRING: THE LABOR

Carson had witnessed pollution in Pittsburgh when she was growing up. Since then, she had been concerned about the negative effects people could have on the environment. As early as 1945, Carson was worried about the dangers that the manmade insecticide DDT posed to wildlife.

Alarming events involving chemicals and the harm they were capable of began to come to light. These motivated Carson to write an entire book about the frightening effects of pesticides on nature; that book was *Silent Spring.*

In this July 1945 image, children play on the beach as workers from Todd Shipyard Corporation run their first public test of an insecticidal fogging machine at Jones Beach in New York. During the test, a four-mile (6.4-km) stretch of beach was blanketed with the DDT fog.

One event that triggered Carson's concern was when her friend Olga Huckins's small bird sanctuary in Duxbury, Massachusetts, was sprayed with DDT. Without Huckins's permission, the government had sprayed her land with the pesticide to kill the mosquitoes.

Huckins wrote to Carson to tell her about the spraying. She said that the birds on her land had died horrible deaths. The DDT had also killed helpful insects. After the spraying, the mosquitoes were still around in large numbers. Huckins asked Carson to use her connections with government officials to stop the spraying. Huckins wrote, "Air spraying where it is not needed or wanted is inhumane, undemocratic, and probably unconstitutional. For those of us who stand helplessly on the tortured earth, it is intolerable."

Another worrisome event was the spraying of DDT on Long Island, New York, to rid the area of gypsy moths. The DDT residue fell everywhere, including on a woman trying to cover her garden and on children playing outdoors. Marjorie Spock and her friend Mary (Polly) Richards had an organic garden and farm animals. Their property was sprayed 14 times in one day. The vegetables were covered in pesticide and ruined. The animals were also exposed to the poison.

Spock and Richards joined together with other Long Island residents, including the well-known ornithologist Robert Cushman Murphy, to sue to stop the spraying of DDT in their area. The case brought together all sorts of experts who testified about the dangers of pesticides. The lawsuit, however, was dismissed on a technicality.

Even so, Carson used many of the experts from the trial as resources for her *Silent Spring* research. For example, she called upon Dr. Malcolm Hargraves, a hematologist from the Mayo Clinic. Hargraves studied pesticides and their link to blood disorders and blood cancer. Also, Carson contacted Morton Biskind, who was an expert about pesticides' effects on human enzymes and on the growth of cancer.

In 1959, a cranberry scare was brought to the public's attention. The herbicide aminotriazole had been approved for cranberry farmers to use after the harvest. However, some growers in Oregon used the herbicide before the harvest and contaminated the cranberries. Scientists had discovered that aminotriazole could cause thyroid cancer in rats. When the public learned of the poisoning of the berries, they stopped buying them. People were becoming aware of the damage pesticides could do.

Carson and the American people saw yet another example of chemical contamination. The radioactive isotope Strontium-90 fell from the skies as part of the fallout after the testing of nuclear weapons. Strontium-90 was later found in cows' milk. Frighteningly, scientists had linked the isotope to leukemia and bone cancer.

While writing *Silent Spring*, Carson had to face terrible emotional and physical challenges. She lost her beloved mother on December 2, 1958. Even though she grieved deeply for Maria, Carson continued to work on the book. She knew that her mother, who had taught her to love the natural world, would want her to fight the dangers of pesticides.

She also had health concerns of her own. Two tumors were discovered in Carson's left breast. In 1946 and 1950, she'd had two other tumors removed from the same breast, and she'd been told they were not cancerous.

Surprisingly, Carson, who was an expert researcher, did not spend much time searching for the most skilled surgeon to operate on her. Carson had the two tumors removed and underwent a radical mastectomy of her left breast in April 1960. After the operation, she asked the doctor if the tumors were malignant. He told her that one was bordering on malignancy, but he did not suggest any other treatment.

Later, Carson would discover that her doctor had lied to her. She found a hard spot on her left side. She wanted another opinion, so she contacted her friend Dr. George Crile of Cleveland. She asked him to look over her medical file. Crile told her she had cancer and that her doctor had kept the diagnosis from her. At that time, a woman's cancer diagnosis was usually discussed with her husband. Because Carson was single, her doctor chose not to tell her that she had breast cancer.

Crile advised Carson to have radiation treatments—advice that she followed. She suffered horrible side effects from the radiation. She had nausea—that is, she felt sick to her stomach—and was exhausted.

One after another, Carson had other physical problems. She was diagnosed with an ulcer. She had a serious staphylococcus infection, a bacterial illness that made her feel close to death. She had arthritis, and the pain in her joints kept her in bed for extended periods of time. She also suffered a bout of iritis, an inflammation of the eye's iris, which caused partial blindness and lasted for weeks. In addition, Carson was found to have angina due to an underlying heart problem.

Despite all these physical ailments, Carson kept up her research and writing. Her research for the book was so thorough that when *Silent Spring* was finished, it had 55 pages of references.

Before *Silent Spring* was published, another chemical scandal hit the news. The drug Thalidomide was prescribed to pregnant women in Europe and Canada. The drug was used to treat morning sickness and insomnia The babies of the women who had taken Thalidomide were born with horrible physical defects.

Thanks to Dr. Frances Kelsey at the U.S. Food and Drug Administration, Thalidomide had not been approved for use in the United States. She had not been satisfied with the drug's safety tests. When speaking to a reporter from *The New York Post*, Carson compared the dangers of Thalidomide and pesticides. "It's all of a piece, Thalidomide and pesticides—they represent our willingness to rush ahead and use something new without knowing what the results are going to be," she said.

SILENT SPRING: THE BIRTH

Silent Spring was serialized in *The New Yorker* beginning on June 2, 1962. The book was published by Houghton Mifflin in September 1962.

In *Silent Spring,* Carson writes that people are part of nature and that using pesticides to control nature is really hurting themselves.

She argues that pesticides are not only killing what they were made to destroy, but they are also killing other plants and animals—and harming people. She wants to have pesticides tested to make sure they are safe for wildlife before use. Carson also hopes to have

Standing in her Silver Spring, Maryland, home library, Rachel Carson holds her book *Silent Spring* in this March 1963 image. Carson said she wanted to bring public attention to the fact that pesticides destroy wildlife and endanger the environment.

pesticide use reduced, especially those, like DDT, that remain in the environment for a long time.

Carson begins the book with a fable about a town that has been exposed to pesticides. White pesticide residue clings to the rooftops of the houses. The birds have died, and various animals and humans have been sickened. No birds sing to welcome the spring season: thus, the book's title—*Silent Spring.*

Pesticides are defined as chemical substances used to destroy all types of "pests." Pesticides include insecticides, for killing insects; herbicides, or weed killer; rodenticides, used on rats and mice; and fungicides, to get rid of fungus.

Farmers use pesticides to kill insects and weeds that damage crops. Their use increases the amount of fruits and vegetables that can be harvested. Public health officials use pesticides to combat diseases transmitted by insects to people, such as malaria and dengue fever. Homeowners use pesticides to rid their lawns of weeds.

Carson explains that there are two major groups of insecticide. DDT is part of the chlorinated hydrocarbons. Carbon atoms are easily joined to atoms of other substances. For example, carbon and hydrogen can be combined. Chemists take the combined carbon and hydrogen molecule and substitute chlorine for one or more of the hydrogen atoms. This forms chlorinated hydrocarbons. The other group of insecticides is organic phosphorus insecticides and includes malathion and parathion.

Carson compares DDT spraying to radioactive particles falling from the sky and poisoning the environment. Her readers understood this idea because they knew that nuclear explosions had radioactive fallout containing dangerous isotopes like Strontium-90.

Carson writes that DDT is a long-lasting insecticide, which stays in the environment for a long time. DDT is fat soluble; therefore, when the pesticide enters an animal's body, it is absorbed into and remains in the fatty tissues of the animals' organs, such as the kidney and liver.

DDT is transferred up the food chain in increasing concentrations. Larger animals eat many of the smaller animals, so they take in more of the DDT. For example, earthworms ingest leaves with DDT on them. Let's say that a little bird eats four earthworms, so the little bird has more DDT in its body than one earthworm had. Finally, a raptor eats two little birds and has more DDT in its body than one little bird had.

Remember that DDT stays in the fatty tissues of animals. Pretend that the little bird eats four DDT contaminated earthworms each day for a week before the raptor eats it. Then, the raptor is eating 28 contaminated earthworms. Since the raptor ate two small birds, he ingested 56 contaminated earthworms. And if the raptor eats two small birds a day for the rest of its life—imagine all the DDT in that raptor!

In *Silent Spring,* Carson discusses many cases in which wildlife has been harmed by pesticides. She also presents well-researched information about how people could be negatively affected by pesticide use. In the Long Island case, DDT sprayed to kill gypsy moths landed on farm produce. People would eat those fruits and vegetables and take DDT into their bodies. Also, the cows that grazed on the grass with DDT residue would produce milk with DDT in it. People would drink this milk and ingest the DDT. That DDT would be absorbed into their fatty tissues. DDT is even found in the breast milk of nursing mothers.

Carson also describes how DDT enters people's drinking water. DDT is sprayed and settles on the soil. The rain washes the pesticide below the ground into a system of underground waters called groundwater. The groundwater is contaminated with DDT. That water flows into streams, rivers, and oceans and finally makes its way to drinking glasses at the kitchen table.

After people take the DDT into their bodies, what might happen? Carson's scientific experts believe that pesticides cause cancer in humans. They also link pesticides and genetic damage in people.

Another surprising way that pesticides might affect people is with the poisoning of bees. Bees pollinate farm crops, but they are often killed by pesticides meant for other insects. If bees do not live to fertilize fruit and vegetable plants, people would not have those foods.

(continues on page 98)

THE MYSTERIOUS DISAPPEARANCE OF THE HONEYBEES

In *Silent Spring,* Rachel Carson warned that pesticides might kill the bee population. She knew this could be a catastrophe because bees fertilize the plants people depend upon for food.

Honeybees (*Apis mellifera*) are responsible for pollinating 90 plant species, such as almonds, strawberries, alfalfa, and even cotton. A honeybee hive has one queen, who can produce up to 2,000 eggs a day. The hive is filled with workers that do specific jobs. The male drones eat and mate with the queen. The nurse bees take care of the young and make sure no bees bring diseases or toxins into the hive. The forager bees collect nectar and pollen from flowers and bring the food back to their fellow bees. As the foragers fly from flower to flower, they spread the pollen and fertilize the plants.

In November 2006, beekeeper David Hackenberg discovered that his honeybees were leaving their hives and not returning. The bees left the queen and young bees behind. They even abandoned the honey. Strangely, no other insects, such as wax moths, moved into the hive or ate the honey, as they normally would have. It was as if they sensed something was wrong.

Beekeepers around the United States and in many parts of the world have experienced bees abandoning their hives. One-third of honeybees in the United States have been lost. The problem is known as colony collapse disorder (CCD).

Scientists don't know what causes CCD. They do know that honeybees do not have good genes for fighting infection or resisting toxins, such as pesticides. The cause of CCD may well be pesticides, as Carson had worried.

The bees in France were suffering CCD. The beekeepers discovered that nearby sunflower fields were being treated with a pesticide called imidacloprid. Imidacloprid interferes with insects' neurological function. The bees were feeding on the sunflowers and ingested the insecticide. The bees exposed to imidacloprid lost their sense of direction and had memory loss. The beekeepers believed that the pesticide was causing the bees to abandon their hives.

The French government has banned the use of imidacloprid. After years, the bee colonies have begun to increase in numbers. As of 2010, the U.S. government has not stopped the use of the imidacloprid.

Interestingly, organic beekeepers have not experienced CCD. They do not use chemical miticides to control mites that kill the bees. These beekeepers move the hives far away from fields that use pesticides, so the bees do not feed on flowers sprayed with pesticides. This is not difficult to do because bees travel only a few miles from their hives.

Pesticides might be the cause of CCD, but scientists are also investigating other possibilities. A virus or fungus might cause CCD. On the other hand, many beehives are transported all around the country to pollinate various crops. This constant movement and resulting stress might contribute to CCD. The scientists are still investigating.

What would happen if there were no honeybees? People would not have as many fruits and vegetables. Even meat and milk would be scarce because the bees wouldn't be around to pollinate the alfalfa that feeds the cattle. Few people would be wearing cotton t-shirts and jeans because bees are needed to pollinate the cotton. It is important for the scientists to keep striving to find the cause of CCD.

(*continued from page 95*)

Many people believe that pesticides are an effective way to kill insects that transmit disease and damage crops. However, as Carson notes in *Silent Spring,* insecticides lose their effectiveness in the long run. Insects become resistant to pesticides. In the case of mosquitoes, for example, certain individual mosquitoes survive pesticide spraying. These mosquitoes live to breed new generations of mosquitoes that are strong enough to survive the pesticides, as well. Soon, there is a population of mosquitoes that cannot be killed by that pesticide. Then, a stronger, more poisonous pesticide needs to be used.

STERILIZING INSECTS

The sterilization of insects can be used to control insect population instead of pesticides. Male insects are exposed to radiation to sterilize them. Then they are released into the wild insect population. These sterilized males compete with the wild males and mate with the wild females. The sterilized males do not fertilize the females' eggs, and no young result. In this way, the population decreases. This technique is called the sterile insect technique (SIT).

Dr. Raymond Bushland and Dr. Edward Knipling first discovered SIT. Their experiments with SIT began in the 1930s. They were trying to eliminate the screwworm fly. Screwworm larvae prey on warm-blooded animals. Screwworms can damage cattle and dairy cows and even kill them. The doctors sterilized the male screwworm flies with radiation and released them into the wild screwworm population. SIT succeeded in eliminating the screwworm in affected areas. Bushland and Knipling won the 1992 World Food Prize for their important work in saving the food supply from the destructive screwworm.

Interestingly, Carson notes that some insects change their behavior to avoid the pesticide and survive. DDT is often sprayed on the interior walls of houses to kill mosquitoes. The mosquitoes stop landing on the sprayed walls. Many even gather outside the home to avoid the pesticide.

There is another reason that pesticides are not effective over a long period of time. Pesticides kill birds. Birds are the natural predators of insects. With the birds gone, the insect population grows.

In *Silent Spring,* Carson presents natural alternatives to pesticide use. She told conservationist Edward O. Wilson that one of her goals for the book was "to build up, in every way I can, the positive

SIT has also been successfully used to control the Mediterranean fruit fly in California. The technique is also being utilized in Africa to fight the tsetse fly, which spreads African sleeping sickness.

Mosquitoes are responsible for infecting people with many deadly diseases, including malaria and dengue fever. Unfortunately, SIT does not work well with mosquitoes. The radiation makes the male mosquitoes weak. When they are released into the regular population, the sterilized males are too weak to compete with the wild males for mating partners.

Because SIT is not effective in controlling mosquito populations, scientists are studying different means to do so. Scientists are experimenting with bacteria called Wolbachia to stop the mosquito that spreads dengue fever. Female mosquitoes infected with Wolbachia have offspring that don't live long enough to pass on dengue fever. If a female mosquito uninfected with Wolbachia mates with an infected male, the female does not produce live offspring. This work looks very promising for the future of natural mosquito control.

alternatives to chemical sprays, for I feel that a book that is wholly against something cannot possibly be as effective as one that points the way to acceptable alternatives."

Carson talks about using natural predators or parasites to kill the destructive "pests." For example, Japanese beetles were destroying plants in the United States. The parasitic wasp preys specifically on the Japanese beetle. This wasp was brought into the country to effectively kill the Japanese beetle. To further control the Japanese beetle, bacteria spores were injected into the soil that would affect only the family of beetles to which the Japanese beetle belonged. These bacteria spores caused "milky disease," which killed Japanese beetle grubs, and successfully reduced the Japanese beetle population.

In *Silent Spring,* Carson also suggests sterilizing male destructive insects so that they can't breed. The sterilization would reduce the population of those insects.

Carson discusses Holland, where natural ways to reduce destructive insects were used with good results. The nematode worm was destroying roses in Holland. The Holland farmers simply planted marigolds near the roses. Marigolds secrete a substance from their roots that is poisonous to the worm. The problem was solved naturally, without pesticides.

Carson's Lasting Impression

Rachel Carson was presented with the Albert Schweitzer Medal from the Animal Welfare Institute in January 1963. She was concerned that animals be treated humanely. Carson worked quietly behind the scenes for animal welfare causes. She didn't want that work to publicly overshadow her main focus— the reduction of pesticide use.

Carson served on the board of directors for Defenders of Wildlife and was a member of the Animal Welfare Institute's advisory board. She also wrote an introduction to the Animal Welfare Institute's booklet *Humane Biology Projects.* In her writing, Carson addressed humane treatment of animals in the science classroom. She said that most animal experiments should be left to the mature scientist and not done by young students.

Carson also wrote the introduction to the book *Animal Machines,* which discussed the inhumane treatment of farm animals. She specifically addressed the terrible existence of animals kept in small, crowded quarters. Carson wrote that those living conditions were unhealthy for the animals because they allowed disease to spread.

To cure and, in some cases, to prevent the animals' illnesses, the farmer would give the animals antibiotics. The overuse of antibiotics caused bacteria that were resistant to antibiotics. The stronger bacteria that survived the antibiotics could find their way to the family dinner table in under-cooked meat. They could also be released into

Rachel Carson poses at her desk in her Maryland home in this 1963 image.

the world through farm runoff that traveled to the earth's waterways and through the air.

In addition, Carson wrote to government officials to protest the use of steel-jawed leghold traps used to catch wild animals. She opposed government programs that used cruel practices, such as deliberate poisoning, to control wildlife predators. Carson also wrote to a congressional committee to champion the ethical treatment of laboratory animals used in scientific studies.

After *Silent Spring* was published, Carson became even more ill. Her breast cancer had spread throughout her body. She underwent radiation therapy to try to stop the cancer. However, she did not attempt chemotherapy. At that time, doctors had just started using chemotherapy to fight cancer, and Carson did not like the idea of allowing untested chemicals inside her body. This is not surprising since she felt the same way about untested chemical pesticides in the environment.

Instead, she decided to try a controversial, but natural, treatment: Krebiozen. Krebiozen was made by injecting mold into a horse's blood and extracting a substance from the blood serum. Carson hoped the Krebiozen would increase her body's resistance to cancer. Unfortunately, this treatment did not seem to help her.

Carson kept her cancer diagnosis private, telling only a few close friends. This was her way, as she had mostly kept her personal life from public view. In her 2005 book *What a Book Can Do: The Publication and Reception of Silent Spring,* author Priscilla Coit Murphy suggests that Carson might have had another reason for staying quiet about her cancer. Perhaps, she did not want the critics to think the links she found between pesticides and cancer were biased by her own experience with the disease.

CONTEMPLATING ETERNITY

Throughout these difficult months, Carson struggled to come to terms with the possibility of her death. She shared her thoughts about

(continues on page 106)

CHEMICAL-FREE FOOD

Rachel Carson was worried that pesticides would reach the dinner tables of people. She believed that it could be harmful to human health for individuals to eat pesticide residue found on food.

Being an educated consumer is good when it comes to chemicals and food. The Environmental Working Group has put together a list of fruits and vegetables that have the most chemical pesticide residue. The list is called the "Dirty Dozen." The foods are peaches, apples, sweet bell peppers, celery, nectarines, strawberries, cherries, lettuce, imported grapes, pears, spinach, and potatoes.

Carson was also concerned about the crowded living conditions of animals raised for food; not only did she view those living conditions as inhumane, but she also worried that, down the line, they might negatively affect the health of people. Animals living close together spread illnesses quickly. Farmers give the animals antibiotics to keep them well. They also use antibiotics to help them grow better. This frequent use of antibiotics causes antibiotic-resistant bacteria—bacteria that are strong enough to survive antibiotics. These bacteria, like *Escherichia coli* (*E. coli*) and salmonella, enter the food system and can reach people if they eat under-cooked meat. It is more difficult to heal these people because the bacteria are so strong.

Many dairy farmers give their cows recombinant bovine growth hormone (rBGH) to increase the amount of milk they produce. The use of rBGH can cause bacterial infections in the cows' udders. Because the cows are making more milk than they naturally would, their bodies can become weakened. Then, they are more likely to become ill. In both cases, the farmers will give antibiotics, which can produce resistant bacteria.

Scientists have discovered a way to change the genes of food plants, using a process called genetic modification. The genes of the plant might be changed so the plant is resistant to insects or has more of certain vitamins. The long-term effects of genetically modified food on humans are not yet known. In the United States, these foods do not have to be labeled as genetically modified.

Eating organic food is a way to avoid most of the chemicals and issues mentioned above. The Organic Foods Production Act was passed by the U.S. Congress in 1990. Foods that are certified 100% organic are grown without chemical pesticides, chemical fertilizers, antibiotics, hormones, or irradiation and are not genetically modified. Eating food without added chemicals seems like a good choice. As an added benefit, some experts believe that organic produce is higher in antioxidants, which fight cancer.

On the other hand, organic food is not without its problems. Natural pesticides are used instead of chemical pesticides. Rotenone is one of these natural pesticides and is extracted from plant root. Rotenone is linked to Parkinson's-like symptoms. Another natural pesticide, pyrethrum, is a possible human carcinogen, a cancer-causing substance.

In addition, chemical fertilizers are not used when growing organic food. Instead, animal feces are used as a natural fertilizer. *E. coli* is often present in animal feces. These bacteria could reach the supper table through organic produce.

When buying prepackaged foods, be careful to avoid chemicals, as well. Look for fewer ingredients on the package and for ingredients with fewer syllables. Remember the "Grandma rule": if your grandmother wouldn't recognize it as food, don't buy it.

(continued from page 103)

eternity with friend Dorothy Freeman. It comforted Carson to know that in death a person's body could contribute to the natural environment. His or her remains would nourish wildlife, just as the remains of ocean's creatures drifted to the lower levels to feed other animals.

Carson was also calmed by the idea that people would remember her through her writing and through the contributions her work had made to the natural world. She wrote to Freeman, "When E.B. White wrote me last summer that he would always think of me when he heard his hermit thrushes, I told him I could think of no more lovely memorial."

Carson did not rule out an afterlife. She found strength in Dr. Crile's concept that death was like "rivers flowing into the sea."

Carson and Freeman spent the summer of 1963 in Maine together. One day, they visited one of their favorite places, the Newagen Inn. There, they observed monarch butterflies on their migration. Later, Carson would reflect on how the monarchs and humans share the natural cycle of life. "For the Monarch, that cycle is measured in a known span of months," she noted in a letter to Freeman. "For ourselves, the measure is something else, the span of which we cannot know. But the thought is the same: when the intangible cycle has run its course it is a natural and not unhappy thing that a life comes to its end."

One of the most difficult aspects of Carson's impending death was the thought of leaving Roger. She knew how many losses he had suffered in his young life. She understood how much her death would affect him.

Before an earlier 1961 trip to California, Carson wrote to Freeman that she intended to take Roger with her. She wrote, "If it must be that his world has to be shattered again before he reaches manhood, at least I want while there is time to share as many 'wonders' as possible with him." Sadly, she was too weak to take Roger when the time came for the California visit.

The idea of Roger being alone was so terrible for Carson to face that she could not bring herself to ask potential guardians if

Rachel Carson (*center*) holds binoculars as she treks through Glover Archbold Park in Washington, D.C., for bird watching with members of the Audubon Society in 1962.

they would raise him. Instead, she named possible guardians in her will.

During October 1963, Carson took a trip to California to speak at the Kaiser Foundation. While she was there, she visited the Pacific Ocean, where she observed hundreds of brown pelicans. These birds had special meaning for her because DDT had negatively affected their population. She also went to Muir Woods. Unhappily, she had to be pushed in a wheelchair, but she was pleased to view the tall, ancient redwood trees.

On December 6, 1963, Carson was inducted into the American Academy of Arts and Letters. This was a prestigious organization, and she was one of only four women who were chosen to be members.

Rachel Carson speaks before the U.S. Senate Government Operations subcommittee, which was studying the effects of pesticide spraying in 1963.

Carson died of a heart attack on April 14, 1964. She had wished to have a small funeral with only close friends in attendance. Unfortunately, her brother Robert ignored her wishes. He planned an elaborate funeral at Washington National Cathedral for April 17, 1964. Nevertheless, Carson's friends, including Dorothy Freeman, Marie Rodell, and Bob Hines, gathered on April 18, 1964, at All Souls Unitarian Church as Carson had wanted. Reverend Duncan Howlett officiated.

In Carson's will, she asked that either Freeman's son, Stanley Freeman Jr., and his wife, Madeleine, or her editor, Paul Brooks, and his wife, Susie, become guardians to Roger. The Freemans declined. Brooks and his wife welcomed Roger into their home.

Carson left generous sums of money from her estate to the Sierra Club and The Nature Conservancy, both conservation groups. Likely, though, her most significant legacy was public awareness of the harm pesticides could cause and an awakening to caring for Earth and its inhabitants. Carson is often considered the mother of the modern environmental movement.

Thanks to *Silent Spring* and the public's newfound concern about the health of the environment, President Richard Nixon established the Environmental Protection Agency (EPA) in 1970. The EPA is responsible for regulating toxins, like pesticides, in the air, water, and soil. In June 1972, DDT was banned for most uses in the United States. Since Carson's death, many state and federal laws have been enacted to protect the environment. For example, the Toxic Substance Control Act was passed in 1976. As of 2010, five chemicals have been restricted by this act.

The DDT ban has helped bring back endangered species that had suffered reproductive problems due to the pesticide's use. As of 2010, the osprey, the brown pelican, the peregrine falcon, and the bald eagle can be found in abundance in the United States.

However, not all people see the stopping of DDT use as beneficial. Critics are harsh when they examine Carson's role in the DDT ban. The critics say that DDT was effective in fighting insect-borne diseases. They blame the reduction in DDT use for causing many preventable deaths.

For example, Angela Logomasini wrote an opinion piece in *The Washington Times* in 2007. She argued that Carson caused unfounded fear about DDT that resulted in its ban. Logomasini wrote, "Today, hundreds of millions of people—mostly African children under five—get seriously ill and more than a million die every year from malaria in large measure because many nations stopped using DDT."

Those who favor the ban often point to the mosquitoes' "behavioral resistance." They say that mosquitoes avoid the interior walls of homes that have been sprayed with DDT. The supporters of the ban say that this proves that DDT was no longer effective against mosquitoes. Donald R. Roberts, professor of the Division of Tropical Public Health at the Uniformed Services University of Health Sciences, says that this is faulty logic. DDT is not only meant to poison mosquitoes, but it also acts as a repellent. When the mosquitoes don't land on the wall, the DDT is doing its repelling job. This way, the people in the home are not bitten.

It is important to remember that Carson did not call for a ban on chemical pesticides. She recommended more testing and a reduction in their use. Her critics often ignore this.

CARSON'S WORK CONTINUES

Soon after Carson's death, Marie Rodell and Shirley Briggs organized The Rachel Carson Trust for the Living Environment, which was renamed the Rachel Carson Council, Inc. in 1978. The Rachel Carson Council helps provide up-to-date information about pesticides to the public.

Carson didn't want people to rely on the government to protect them from environmental hazards. She wanted individuals to take responsibility for their own welfare; today, the Rachel Carson Council can act as their resource. In a 1962 *Life* magazine article, Carson said, "People say we wouldn't be allowed to use . . . [pesticides] if they were dangerous. It just isn't so. Trusting so-called authorities is not enough. A sense of personal responsibility is what we desperately need."

A salt marsh next at the Rachel Carson National Wildlife Refuge in Maine is a good spot for bird watching. The Mousam River is visible on the right.

Let's say a person lives near an apple orchard that is being sprayed with chemical pesticides. That individual can telephone the Rachel Carson Council with his concerns. The organization will contact the apple grower and ask what type of pesticide is being used. Then, the group will let the individual know and outline the risks associated with the pesticide. The council will even discuss natural alternatives to the pesticide.

The Rachel Carson Council also has published a booklet discussing organic golf courses. Golf courses that are maintained with chemical pesticides pose hazards to wildlife, course employees, and players. The publication describes the success of two organic golf courses and offers steps to keep a pesticide-free course.

During her lifetime, Carson had hoped to purchase land near her home in Maine to be used as a nature preserve. She wanted people to have the opportunity to experience the same wonder and peace that Maine's natural environment offered her. Unfortunately, she couldn't afford to do this.

After Carson's death, others helped make her dream a reality. The Rachel Carson National Wildlife Refuge consists of approximately 5,500 acres (2,226 hectares) in Maine. The goal of the refuge is to preserve federally endangered species, such as the Atlantic Coast piping plover, a shorebird. The refuge also protects species endangered in Maine, such as the New England cottontail rabbit.

The refuge is actively managed to give these animals a livable habitat. Park rangers maintain low shrubs as cottontail living space. The cottontail eats, breeds, and hides from predators in this thicket. The refuge employees rope off portions of the Maine beach when it is nesting time for the plover. In this way, the birds and their nests won't be disturbed.

The park rangers and volunteers eliminate invasive plants, so the animals' natural food can grow in large amounts. They also plant more of the vegetation the animals need for nutrition. These new plants have the added benefit of crowding out the invasive plant species in the long run.

Another organization that continues Carson's work is The Rachel Carson Homestead Association. The association is located at Carson's childhood home in Springdale, Pennsylvania. The organization teaches visitors about Carson's life and her ecological mission. Programs are offered so the public can learn about the natural animal and plant life in that area.

The group advises companies in ways they can be more environmentally responsible. These companies commit to polluting less and to conserving energy.

The Rachel Carson Homestead also provides information about making chemical-free decisions in everyday life. It encourages individuals to choose food without pesticides and to use chemical-free products, such as cosmetics without formaldehyde and paraben.

Every year, the Rachel Carson Homestead hosts Rachel's Sustainable Feast. Local organic food is served. Participants are asked to bring reusable water bottles. At the feast, attendees learn

ENDOCRINE-DISRUPTING CHEMICALS

As of 2010, there are 80,000 chemicals being used in the United States. Pesticides are required by federal law to undergo safety testing, but there are no required federal safety tests for industrial chemicals. Some of these chemicals are considered to be endocrine disrupters. Endocrine disruptors act like hormones in the body or block the body's hormones.

Scientists are investigating endocrine disruptors to see if they are linked to human illnesses or disorders. They are studying links between disruptor chemicals and certain breast cancers that grow faster with estrogen present. Experts are also looking into these chemicals and their possible relationship to early puberty in females. In males, the scientists are investigating a connection between endocrine disruptors and low sperm count, undescended testicles, and testicular cancer.

Where are these endocrine disruptors found? They are found in pesticides, such as DDT and the herbicide atrazine. Chemicals that are used in plastics to make them flexible, like phthalates, are considered endocrine disruptors. Phthalates are contained in certain plastic food wraps and children's soft toys. The endocrine disruptor Bisphenol-A is added to hard plastic, like some baby bottles and water bottles. Parabens in cosmetic items are being investigated as endocrine-disrupting chemicals.

As scientists continue their research into endocrine disruptors, individuals can consider avoiding products with these chemicals added.

about environmentally friendly practices, such as recycling and composting.

Carson's book *The Sense of Wonder,* based on her earlier *Woman's Home Companion* article, was published in 1965, after her death. Carson would have been pleased. She wanted parents to encourage their children to experience joy in wildlife. All her life, Carson had found peace and hope through nature. In the book, she wrote, "There is symbolic as well as actual beauty in the migration of the birds, the ebb and flow of the tides, the folded bud ready for the spring. There is something infinitely healing in the repeated refrains of nature—the assurance that dawn comes after night, and spring after the winter."

Rachel Carson was posthumously awarded the Presidential Medal of Freedom by President Jimmy Carter in 1980. The Presidential Medal of Freedom is the highest civilian award and is given to ". . . individuals who make an especially meritorious contribution to the security or national interests of the United States, world peace, cultural or other significant public or private endeavors." Carson's contributions to the environment and the creatures that inhabit it likely will be remembered for generations to come.

How to Get Involved

These conservation organizations provide information and offer opportunities to get involved.

Animal Welfare Institute

900 Pennsylvania Ave SE

Washington, D.C. 20003

http://www.awionline.org/

Rachel Carson was a supporter of the Animal Welfare Institute. This organization fights to have animals treated humanely. The group's Web site explains animal welfare laws that are being considered by Congress. Individuals are encouraged to write their government officials to help get the laws passed. The Animal Welfare Institute also offers free educational brochures, such as *Sharks at Risk.*

Bat Conservation International

P.O. Box 162603

Austin, Texas 78716

http://batcon.org/

Bat Conservation International is devoted to keeping bat populations abundant. Visit the organization's Web site to learn lots of fascinating facts about bats. Since many bats are insect-eaters, they act as natural alternatives to chemical pesticides. Bat Conservation International encourages individuals to build bat houses and offers bat house construction plans.

MarineBio.org, Inc.

P.O. Box 235273

Encinitas, California 92023

http://Marinebio.org/

MarineBio is dedicated to conserving the world's oceans. The group's Web site offers a magical view of the oceans and its inhabitants. It gives site visitors tips about keeping the oceans clean and livable for the sea plants and animals.

World Wildlife Fund
1250 Twenty-Fourth St. NW
P.O. Box 97180
Washington, D.C. 20090-7180
http://worldwildlifefund.org/
World Wildlife Fund helps to conserve the world's endangered species. Learn about endangered species, like the tiger and the giant panda, through informative fact sheets. Web site visitors can become involved by adopting an endangered animal.

Chronology

May 27, 1907	Rachel Carson is born in Springdale, Pennsylvania.
September 1918	Carson's first story is published in *St. Nicholas* League.
June 10, 1929	Carson graduates magna cum laude from Pennsylvania College for Women.
July 1929	Carson sees the ocean for the first time and works at the Marine Biological Laboratory in Woods Hole as a beginning investigator.
June 14, 1932	Carson graduates from The Johns Hopkins University with a master's degree in zoology.
August 17, 1936	Carson is hired as a junior aquatic biologist at the U.S. Bureau of Fisheries.
January 1937	Carson's sister Marion dies, and Carson and her mother, Maria, take responsibility for raising Marion's two daughters.
November 1, 1941	Carson's first book, *Under the Sea Wind,* is published.
July 15, 1945	Carson asks *Reader's Digest* editors if they want an article about the negative effects of DDT on wildlife. They reject the query.
July 2, 1951	*The Sea Around Us* is published.
January 27, 1952	Carson is awarded the prestigious National Book Award for nonfiction.
April 7, 1952	Carson wins the John Burroughs Medal for "nature book of literary merit."

October 1955	*The Edge of the Sea* is published.
January 30, 1957	Carson's niece Marjorie dies. Soon after, she adopts her grandnephew Roger.
September 27, 1962	*Silent Spring* is published.
January 26, 1963	Carson testifies about pesticides before the President's Science Advisory Committee.
April 3, 1963	Carson appears on *CBS Reports* to share her research on pesticide hazards.
June 4, 1963	Carson testifies before Senator Ribicoff's subcommittee and offers recommendations for avoiding the dangers of pesticides.
December 6, 1963	Carson is inducted into the American Academy of Arts and Letters.
April 14, 1964	Carson dies of a heart attack.
1965	*The Sense of Wonder* is published posthumously.
June 9, 1980	President Jimmy Carter awards Carson the Presidential Medal of Freedom posthumously.

Glossary

bioluminescence   A chemical reaction in which an animal makes its own light

chlorinated hydrocarbon   A combined carbon and hydrogen molecule in which at least one chlorine atom is substituted for a hydrogen atom

cirrus clouds   Clouds that are high-flying and wispy in appearance; they are usually composed of ice crystals

conservationist   A person who preserves and protects natural resources

cumulus clouds   Clouds that have the appearance of fluffy balls of cotton; they are formed when hot air rises, and then cools and condenses.

dinoflagellates   Single-celled aquatic organisms

echolocation   The use of sound waves to find objects and to navigate

ecologist   A scientist who studies organisms and their relationship to their environment

food chain   A model that shows how energy is passed, as food, from one organism to another; for example, fish eat plankton, and then birds eat the fish.

fungicide   A chemical substance used to kill fungus

habitat   A plant or an animal's natural environment; the place where a plant or an animal lives

herbicide   A chemical substance used to kill plants, especially weeds

insecticide   A chemical substance used to kill insects, such as mosquitoes and lice

marine biologist   A scientist who studies plants and animals in the ocean or in a waterway connecting to the sea

optimistic   A word that means "to anticipate a positive outcome"

parasitology   The study of organisms that survive on or in host organisms

pesticides   Chemical substances used to kill pests, such as insects and weeds

rodenticide   A chemical substance used to kill rodents, such as mice and rats

stratus clouds   Clouds that are low-flying and usually gray in color

Thalidomide   A drug that was prescribed in the late 1950s to pregnant women to combat morning sickness; the drug caused severe birth defects in the babies of the pregnant women who took it.

wildlife refuge   A protected living area for animals

zoology   A branch of biology devoted to the study of animals

Bibliography

Bat Conservation International. "Benefits of Bats." Available online. URL: http://www.batcon.org/index.php/all-about-bats/intro-to-bats/sub category/18.html. Accessed April 26, 2010.

Bat World Sanctuary. "Myths and Facts." Available online. URL: http:// batworld.org/myths_facts/myths_facts.html. Accessed April 26, 2010.

Bekoff, Mark and Jan Nystrum. "The Other Side of Silence: Rachel Carson's Views on Animals." *Zygon: Journal of Religion & Science* 39, no.4 (December 2004). Available online. URL: http://web.ebscohost.com. proxy.library.emory.edu/ehost/pdf?vid=2&hid=2&sid=093b81eb-645c-4116-8418-f1fd39ec9797%40sessionmgr10. Accessed April 25, 2010.

Benjamin, Allison and Brian McCallum. *A World Without Bees.* New York: Pegasus Books, 2009.

Blatt, Harvey. *What You Don't Know About What You Eat.* Cambridge, Massachusetts: The MIT Press, 2008.

Briggs, Shirley A. *Basic Guide to Pesticides: Their Characteristics and Hazards.* Washington: Hemisphere Publishing Corporation, 1992.

Brooks, Paul. *The House of Life: Rachel Carson at Work.* Boston, Massachusetts: Houghton Mifflin Company, 1972.

Brown, Dorothy M. *American Women in the 1920s: Setting a Course.* Boston, Massachusetts: Twayne Publishers, 1989.

Carson, Rachel. "A Battle in the Clouds." *St. Nicholas* League, September 1918. Rachel Carson Papers, Yale Collection of American Literature, Beinecke Rare Book and Manuscript Library, Yale University. Available online. URL: http://beinecke.library.yale.edu/dl_crosscollex/brbldl/one ITEM.asp?pid=2003110&iid=1013352&srchtype. Accessed April 26, 2010.

———. *Conservation in Action.* 5 booklets. Washington, D.C.: U.S. Fish and Wildlife Service, 1947–1950. Available online. URL: http:// training.fws.gov/history/historicdocuments.html. Accessed April 26, 2010.

————. *The Edge of the Sea.* Boston, Massachusetts: Houghton Mifflin Company, 1955.

————. "Letter to Raymond Brown." October 15, 1946. Rachel Carson Papers, Yale Collection of American Literature, Beinecke Rare Book and Manuscript Library, Yale University. Available online. URL: http://beinecke.library.yale.edu/dl_crosscollex/brbldl/oneITEM.asp?pid=2026500&iid=1096585&srchtype. Accessed April 26, 2010.

————. *The Sea Around Us.* New York: Oxford University Press, 2003 edition.

————. *The Sense of Wonder.* New York: Harper & Row, 1998 edition.

————. *Silent Spring.* Boston, Massachusetts: Houghton Mifflin Company, 1962.

————. "Teach Your Child to Wonder." *Woman's Home Companion,* July 1956. Available online. URL: http://www.fws.gov/digitalmedia/cgi-bin/showfile.exe?CISOROOT=/natdiglib&CISOPTR=8512&filename=8513.pdf. Accessed April 26, 2010.

————. *Under the Sea Wind.* New York: Oxford University Press, 1952 edition.

City-Data.com. "Pittsburgh: History." Available online. URL: http://www.city-data.com/us-cities/The-Northeast/Pittsburgh-History.html. Accessed April 26, 2010.

Couric, Katie. "Animal Antibiotics Overuse Hurting Humans?" *CBS News,* February 9, 2010. Available online. URL: http://www.cbsnews.com/stories/2010/02/09/eveningnews/main6191530.shtml. Accessed April 26, 2010.

DeMarco, Patricia M., Ph.D. (executive director, Rachel Carson Homestead Association), Telephone interview with the author, March 14, 2010.

Dunlap, Thomas R. ed. *DDT, Silent Spring and the Rise of Environmentalism.* Seattle, Washington: University of Washington Press, 2008.

Easton, Thomas. ed. *Taking Sides: Clashing Views on Environmental Issues.* Boston, Massachusetts: McGraw-Hill Higher Education, 2010.

Forman, Lillian E. *Genetically Modified Foods*. Edina, Minnesota: ABDO Publishing Company, 2010.

Freeman, Martha, ed. *Always Rachel: The Letters of Rachel Carson and Dorothy Freeman 1952–1964: An Intimate Portrait of a Remarkable Friendship*. Boston, Massachusetts: Beacon Press, 1995.

Galbraith, John Kenneth. *The Great Crash 1929*. Boston, Massachusetts: Marine Books by Houghton Mifflin Company. 1997 edition.

Gore, Albert. "Introduction to *Silent Spring*." *Silent Spring*. Boston, Massachusetts: Houghton Mifflin Company, 1994 edition. Available online. URL: http://clinton2.nara.gov/WH/EOP/OVP/24hours/carson. html. Accessed April 26, 2010.

Gould, Carol Grant. *The Remarkable Life of William Beebe: Explorer and Naturalist*. Washington: Island Press, 2004.

Gow, Mary. *The Stock Market Crash of 1929: Dawn of the Great Depression*. Berkeley Heights, New Jersey: Enslow Publishers, Inc. 2003.

Graham, Frank, Jr. *Since Silent Spring*. Boston, Massachusetts: Houghton Mifflin Company, 1970.

Harris, Tom. "How Bats Work: Bats and Echolocation." *How Stuff Works*. Available online: URL: http://animals.howstuffworks.com/mammals/ bat2.htm. Accessed April 26, 2010.

Heinz Meng, interview by Lynn Spangler. *On Campus at SUNY New Paltz*, UMA Production, ©2001.

Hirschmann, Kris. *The Magic School Bus: Bats*. New York: Scholastic, Inc., 2001.

Kaufman, John and Heinz Meng. *Falcons Return: Restoring an Endangered Species*. Unionvale, New York: KAV Books, 1992.

Kerr, Jim. *Food: Ethical Debates on What We Eat*. Mankato, Minnesota: Smart Apple Media, 2009.

Lear, Linda. (author of *Rachel Carson: Witness for Nature*), E-mail interviews with the author, April 6, 2010 and April 21, 2010.

———, ed. *Lost Woods: The Discovered Writing of Rachel Carson*. Boston, Massachusetts: Beacon Press, 1998.

————. *Rachel Carson: Witness for Nature.* New York: Henry Holt and Company, 1997.

Lemelson-MIT Program. "William Beebe Underwater Exploration." April 2002. Available online. URL: http://web.mit.edu/invent/iow/beebe.html. Accessed April 26, 2010.

Logomasini, Angela. "Rachel Carson's Deadly Legacy." *The Washington Times,* May 31, 2007. Available online. URL: http://cei.org/gencon/019,05945.cfm. Accessed April 26, 2010.

Marine Biological Laboratory. "Discover the MBL." Available online. URL: http://www.mbl.edu/about/discovery/index.html. Accessed April 26, 2010.

Matson, Brad. *The Incredible Record-Setting Deep-Sea Dive of the Bathysphere.* Berkeley Heights, New Jersey: Enslow Publishing, Inc., 2003.

Murphy, Priscilla Coit. *What a Book Can Do: The Publication of Silent Spring.* Amherst, Massachusetts: University of Massachusetts Press, 2005.

The New York Times. "Rachel Carson Dies of Cancer, 'Silent Spring' Author was 56." April 15, 1964. Available online. URL: http://www.nytimes.com/learning/general/onthisday/bday/0527.html. Accessed April 26, 2010.

The Nobel Foundation. "Albert Schweitzer: The Nobel Peace Prize 1932." Available online. URL: http://nobelprize.org/nobel_prizes/peace/laureates/1952/schweitzer-bio.html. Accessed April 26, 2010.

O'Brien, Robyn with Rachel Kranz. *The Unhealthy Truth: How Our Food Is Making Us Sick and What We Can Do About It.* New York: Broadway Books, 2009.

Official Site of the International Albert Schweitzer Association. "Biographie lange: Albert Schweitzer 1875–1965." Available online. URL: http://www.schweitzer.org/index.php?option=com_content&view=category&layout=blog&id=60&Itemid=57&lang=en. Accessed April 26, 2010.

Ohio State University Department of History. "Clash of Cultures in the 1910s and 1920s: The New Woman: Work, Education, and Reform." Available online. URL: http://ehistory.osu.edu/osu/mmh/clash/NewWoman/ workeducationreform-page1.htm. Accessed April 26,2010.

PBS: The American Experience. "William Beebe: Going Deeper." Available online. URL: http://www.pbs.org/wgbh/amex/ice/sfeature/beebe. html. Accessed April 26, 2010.

Post, Diana (president, Rachel Carson Council, Inc.), Telephone interview with the author, April 19, 2010.

Presnall, Judith Janda. *The Importance of Rachel Carson.* San Diego, California: Lucent Books, 1995.

Richardson, Phil. *Bats.* Washington, D.C.: Smithsonian Institution Press, 2002.

Ring, Elizabeth. *Rachel Carson: Caring for the Earth.* Connecticut: The Millbrook Press, 1992.

Roosevelt, Tweed. "Theodore Roosevelt: A Brief Biography." Theodore Roosevelt Association, 2003. Available online. URL: http://www. theodoreroosevelt.org/life/biotr.htm. Accessed July 10, 2010

Ryan, Aileen (biochemist), Telephone interview with the author, April 11, 2010.

Scanlon, Deborah G. "Summers in Woods Hole Spur Rachel Carson's Love of Ocean." *Falmouth Enterprise,* June 8, 2007. Available online. URL: http://www.mbl.edu/news/features/pdf/carson_article_scanlon. pdf. Accessed April 26, 2010.

Schacker, Michael. *A Spring Without Bees: How Colony Collapse Disorder Has Endangered Our Food Supply.* Guilford, Connecticut: The Lyons Press, 2008.

Schwaab, Karrie (park ranger, Rachel Carson National Wildlife Refuge). Telephone interview with the author, April 13, 2010.

Sideris, Lisa H. and Kathleen Dean Moore. *Rachel Carson: Legacy and Challenge.* Albany, New York: State University of Albany Press, 2008.

Sogin, Mitchell L. (director, Josephine Bay Paul Center for Comparative Molecular Biology and Evolution). E-mail correspondence with the author, July 6, 2010.

Steingraber, Sandra. *Living Downstream.* New York: Vintage Books, 1997.

Sterling, Philip. *Sea and Earth: The Life of Rachel Carson.* New York: Thomas Y. Crowell Company, 1970.

Strickland, Eliza. "Biologists Evolve Mosquito-Killing Bacteria to Fight Dengue Fever." *Discover,* January 5, 2009. Available online. URL: http://blogs.discovermagazine.com/80beats/2009/01/05/biologists-evolve-a-mosquito-killing-bacteria-to-fight-dengue-fever/. Accessed April 26, 2010.

United States Fish and Wildlife Services. "Rachel Carson: A Conservation Legacy." Available online. URL: http://www.fws.gov/rachelcarson/. Accessed April 26, 2010.

Weir, Kirsten. "Rachel Carson's Birthday Bashing." *Salon,* January 29, 2007. Available online. URL: http://www.salon.com/news/feature/2007/06/29/rachel_carson/index.html. Accessed April 26, 2010.

The White House Office of the Press Secretary. "President Obama Names Medal of Freedom Recipients: 16 Agents of Change to Receive Top Civilian Honors." July 30, 2009. Available online. URL: http://www.whitehouse.gov/the_press_office/President-Obama-Names-Medal-of-Freedom-Recipients/. Accessed July 14, 2010.

Whitman, Sylvia. *V is for Victory: The American Homefront during World War II.* Minneapolis, Minnesota: Lerner Publications, 1993.

The World Food Prize. "Dr. Edward R. Knipling Dr. Raymond C. Bushland: 1992 World Food Laureates." Available online. URL: http://www.worldfoodprize.org/laureates/Past/1992.htm. Accessed April 26, 2010.

Further Resources

Collard, Sneed B. III. *In the Deep Sea.* Tarrytown, New York: Marshall Cavendish Benchmark, 2006.

Gow, Mary. *Rachel Carson: Ecologist and Activist.* Berkeley Heights, New Jersey, 2005.

Levine, Ellen. *Up Close: Rachel Carson.* New York: Viking, 2007.

Lytle, Mark Hamilton. *The Gentle Subversive: Rachel Carson, Silent Spring, and the Rise of the Environmental Movement.* New York: Oxford University Press, 2007.

Piddock, Charles. *Rachel Carson: A Voice for the Natural World.* Pleasantville, New York: Gareth Stevens Publishing, 2009.

Scherer, Glenn and Marty Fletcher. *Who on Earth is Rachel Carson?* Berkeley Heights, New Jersey: Enslow Publishers, 2009.

WEB SITES

Rachel Carson

http://rachelcarson.org/

Linda Lear, author of *Rachel Carson: Witness for Nature,* has created this Web site. Discover more about Rachel Carson's life. This site is rich with additional facts about Carson and has many Internet links useful for further research.

Rachel Carson Council, Inc.

http://www.rachelcarsoncouncil.org/

Rachel Carson sounded the alarm about the harm pesticides could do. Find out about chemicals that are still causing concern and about what is being done to reduce pesticide use today.

Rachel Carson Homestead Association

http://www.rachelcarsonhomestead.org/

Explore Rachel Carson's life, childhood, and home. Find tips for earth-friendly practices. Sign the Rachel Carson Legacy Challenge.

Rachel Carson National Wildlife Refuge

http://www.fws.gov/northeast/rachelcarson/

This Web site is devoted to the nearly 5,500 acres (2,226 hectares) named for Carson. Learn about what is being done to protect the endangered species on this Maine refuge.

Picture Credits

Index

About the Author

MARIE-THERESE MILLER holds a bachelor's degree in psychology and a master's degree in writing from Manhattanville College. She is the author of the Dog Tales book series: *Distinguished Dogs, Helping Dogs, Hunting and Herding Dogs, Police Dogs,* and *Search and Rescue Dogs* (Chelsea Clubhouse, 2007). In addition, Chelsea House published her book *Managing Responsibilities* in 2009, as part of its Character Education series. Miller has written more than 100 nonfiction articles, including "Panic," which can be found in *Chicken Soup for the Soul: Preteen Soul 2* and *Chicken Soup for the Soul: Teens Talk Tough Times.*

Miller and Rachel Carson share a love of the ocean. Each summer, Miller, her husband, John, and their five children visit Cape May, New Jersey, to collect seashells, watch dolphins, and jump the waves. During the rest of the year, she lives with her family in upstate New York. Please visit her Web site at www.marie-theresemiller.com